Suicide for Beginners" (Volume 2)

by

Martyn Langdale

SUICIDE FOR BEGINNERS (VOLUME 2)

PREFACE

In January 2007 my wife and girlfriend were not really getting along, more importantly, neither of them was getting along with me. Call me naive but I had an inkling that the situation was becoming a touch heated, with the benefit of a grammar school education, and an aversion to pain, especially pain involving me, together with a desire to maintain my testicles in the position to which they had become accustomed over the past four decades, I decided that I needed a master plan to preserve what little sanity/self respect I had manage to retain. I decided to 'lie low' in Thailand for a while in order to escape, regroup and gather my thoughts, in so doing, I was possibly the only man in history to visit this den of depravity in an attempt to get away from the female of the species.

Within a week, my devoted girlfriend had jumped between the sheets/desk/compost heap with another poor unfortunate, who just happened to have a cock he wasn't using, which precipitated my breakdown 6500 miles from home with nobody but ladyboys for comfort. Still, this was more solace than was available to my accountant and solicitor who both promptly followed suit and came out in sympathy, after considering the financial implications of my errant ways. Eventually, I limped home to Blighty where my darling wife, ever the understanding one, attempted to pick up the pieces of my hitherto illustrious career and put my broken head together again. I was, in short, a physical and emotional wreck.

To compound my problems, shortly after my return the Harley motorcycle, which I rode every day, decided to have its own breakdown, precipitated by its unhealthy alliance with a local hedge, at a velocity which was not conducive to my longevity, and proceeded at a rate of knots to plough through the aforementioned obstacle and adjacent field, despite my protestations and limited pain threshold, towards the general direction of its worried bovine residents.

The upshot of my off roading activities, on a vehicle hardly designed for such agricultural exertions, (although some bikers would beg to differ), was a two month sabbatical in the spinal injuries unit in Sheffield's Northern General hospital, where the surgeons welded, bolted and stitched my shattered body back together again. With very little effort on my part, I had succeeded in fracturing my spine in four places, paralysed my left arm and my right arm resembled the shittiest jigsaw that Waddingtons had ever produced.To compound the situation, I was reduced to eating and breathing through a tube, (not the same one) and pissing into a hot water bottle via an unceremoniously, rammed hosepipe, which would, I later discovered to my cost, would result in me, forever pissing in two directions simultaneously and necessitate the use of the sit down, forward facing urination method. I did however find this method somewhat easier than the advanced yoga/acrobatics which would have otherwise been required in order to leave me and the surrounding area piss free.

The upside of the altercation was that, due to the copious amounts of titanium/stainless steel involved in my rebuilding, I was now worth considerably more on the open scrap market. The bike meanwhile, escaped little better than my body, since it was declared a write off, which I considered to be less than it deserved, as I blamed the overweight piece of American shit, rather than any lack of judgement or experience on my part.

Four years down the line, I am as good as I will get, I still own my real ale pub. Unfortunately, my years as a pro musician seem to be at an end, due in no small part to my paralysis and reliance on controlled drugs. Similarly, any modelling aspirations, which up to this point in my life I might have harboured, seem to be behind me now and have, to coin a phrase, gone down the pan on the way to the shitworks of oblivion.

Here is my story of a defining period in my life wot I writted in order to make a scintilla of sense from the car crash/fuckup that will hence fourth and forever more, be known as my life. Hope it makes you laugh and shit yourself in equal quantities.

Regards Martyn.

For Brian, Don and Ady, the one legged pigeons of Gainsborough who's welfare I have made my concern for the past decade, not because I like pigeons but because I like to piss off the parasitic leaches of West Lindsey District Council and their bureaucratic ways.

Thanks to my ever-loving wife for always being there.

You are a diamond.

ASBO'S AND BEER

It was a beautiful, cloudless spring day as I rode the Harley from Lincoln back to Gainsborough town, I had bought a tin of pipe tobacco from my favourite vendor and parked the bike adjacent to the end of RAF Scampton runway, if truth be known, next to the thoughtfully provided, publicly financed council amenity that was the 'dogging site', uniquely, in the area, not only a place to hone one's personal depths of depravity/semen slinging abilities, but also a prime location to observe the practise sessions of the world famous Red Arrows display team. I never cease to be awestruck by the abilities of these guys, who in my opinion, are the best in the world, and worthy ambassadors of all that was once good about team GB. Thirty minutes later, as the team prepared to land, and duly sated from the eternal pleasure of a pipe full of freshly opened tobacco, sadly one of the few legal disgusting habits which does not involve controlled drugs/Marigold gloves which is still available to me, I knocked the remnants of the bowl out on a nearby tree stump, tucked the pipe inside my breast pocket, donned my lid and set off down the A 1500 for home. This road was built by the Romans whilst they were over here educating us heathens of the virtues of sanitation and the hypocaust system and the pleasures of Domino's pizzas and mozzarella, whilst administering a good beating, with no doubt copious amounts of 'stds' and illegitimate big nosed offspring/wives of a disproportionate arse/belly/waist configuration. The road must have been built early in their attempt at world domination since, apparently, they had yet to learn the skill of making corners, which must have been a real fucker if any obstacles were in the way. Tillbridge lane, as the two thousand year old feat of engineering is titled, runs straight as Dirk Diggler's rampant member whilst perusing the lingerie section of the Grattan's spring catalogue, it is surrounded by nothingness and fields but is a favourite of the local bikers and over exuberant traffic police in equal measures of enthusiasm. Suddenly, I became aware that the cool breeze, which I was enjoying around my torso, via the half opened jacket zip, had turned into a searing heat. To exacerbate the situation, I appeared to by trying to emulate my heroes by leaving my own smoke trail, which by now was drifting across the Lincolnshire fields. I tentatively glanced down to see the antique Davy lamp, which I had purchased earlier and had been thoughtfully wrapped in newspaper by the shop, albeit in a ridiculous quantity of the eminently combustible material/kindling.The jacket inferno, with the aid of the rebellious pipe was now well and truly alight, and was now seriously threatening my welfare and my ability to produce babies. I instinctively slammed on the anchors, threw the bike onto the grass verge and started to strip off my burning clothes, before jumping up and down on the flaming mess that hitherto had been my wardrobe, as one does, in a vain and futile attempt to extinguish what was by now quite a respectable bonfire, in truth it would have had Ray Mears shitting himself with envy.

Tillbridge lane is in the middle of nowhere, has few dwellings other than the odd farmhouse and has about as many pedestrians as Rolf Harris has female friends under the age of twelve, in short, the only reason to go near it is if you have a tractor or a latent fetish for sheep. How very fortuitous then that the only young mother and daughter for twenty miles around should be walking in that exact spot at the very moment I chose to combust. How very lucky that they should pass just at the moment that the middle aged lunatic proceeded to strip half naked and stamp on his discarded smouldering vestments in an apparent fit of rage and utter stupidity. If my memory serves me well, her words were,' come away from the bad man darling, he's a fucking idiot', before she turned toward the direction of Lincoln and promptly 'legged it', whilst muttering about perverts, Rampton and medication

I consoled myself by examining the remains of what, five minutes earlier, had been my expensive jacket, Harley t shirt and various charred pieces of Lincolnshire Today. The welded plastic and leather which had hitherto been my wallet and credit cards,together with my Rayban's and money where now but charred memories. It had been an expensive morning which had left me nursing a seared chest, which, if given a few more seconds on gas mark 5 would have necessitated a trip to the local A and E and left me with a chest like Nicki Lauda's ear. Obviously, none of these tribulations prevented my customers from taking the piss upon my return to the pub where I had the appearance of a Terminator stuntman who was not particularly good at his job, next time I would ensure that the pipe was properly extinguished before riding, alas this would not be the last time that this two wheeled conveyance would cause me pain and suffering.

."'You can fuck Off" I growled in the general direction of the police officer as he started to climb out of the patrol car. "You're no good to me now, get back in your car and fuck off". This was not my usual approach when dealing with an officer of the law, but then it wasn't every day that I was physically and verbally abused by three drunken members of the local fortune telling and scrap dealing caravan owners club, who had decided that it was perfectly acceptable to gate crash a private barbecue, which I had organised for family and customers of the pub, which I owned. Apparently, they had figured that I was the only obstruction to them obtaining a free dinner, at my expense, and had thus deemed it perfectly reasonable to render me unconscious. It had taken the officer in question some forty five minutes to respond to a 999 call, in the centre of town, half a mile from the police station. "Last week I received a speeding ticket and it arrived before you did", I sarcastically remarked to the boy in blue, "now piss off. I don't want to talk to you". I was not a happy bunny and had decided that in the interests of keeping my liquor licence, not to mention my liberty, it would be better for all parties if the officer in question left immediately. "You can't speak to me like that" he retorted, seemingly oblivious to the fact that I just had, at which point I reminded him that this was only the second occasion in fifteen years, that it had been necessary to seek the assistance of the local constabulary. This was an impressive record for any town centre pub, but in this particular town it was nothing short of a minor miracle. Furthermore, I made it patently clear that in no way was I satisfied with his lacklustre response, at which point he dutifully pissed off – RESULT!!

I had bought the pub some four years previously. It was a well respected, award winning, real ale house resplendent with eight hand pumps serving ales from small independent brewers together with fine wines, lagers and leg nobbling ciders, whose ABV's were somewhat more impressive than the England cricket teams test scores. The pub was a beautiful three hundred year old, grade II Listed maltings, which had been converted by the previous owner and stood in the quiet picturesque fishing hamlet of Gainsborough, Lincolnshire, on the tranquil idyllic banks of the river Trent. Those of you who are familiar with the area, will realise that I am apt to use a certain degree of poetic licence when describing this small market town, which in truth is to idyllic, what Myra Hindley was to the childminding profession. If any town was blessed with the sad misfortune to be twinned with this abject shithole it would undoubtedly be situated in a literal and metaphorical desert, Helmland Province springs to mind, somewhere inviting and friendly, such as Camp Bastion, even Kate Adie in full body armour would be reticent to set foot into Gainsborough's civic boundaries.

Gainsborough was once a proud inland port, the largest in the country in fact, it is situated some twenty miles east of Lincoln and for decades had a reputation as a centre of engineering excellence. It was home to two major industries, Roses, who manufactured packing machinery, which was exported across the globe to such customers as the tea plantations in the colonies and for Mr Cadbury's chocolate factories, hence the name of the chocolates, and Marshalls, the renowned boiler and tractor manufacturers who produced steam and traction engines including the famous Field Marshall tractors. Both factories had turned their skills to arms production during the war years and had made guns, tanks, submarines and turrets for the famous Lancaster bombers, many of which were based in Lincolnshire earning the area the title 'Bomber County'. Some of the Lancasters were based at nearby RAF Scampton, now the home of the revered 'Red Arrows' display team. In May 1943, 617 squadron, who subsequently became known as the 'Dambusters' launched 'Operation Chastise' from Scampton airbase. Under the command of Wing Commander Guy Gibson, the aircrews attacked the Mohne, Sorpe and Eder dams with Barnes Wallis's famous bouncing bomb, thus delivering a massive blow to the German industrial machine and the German morale, even today the raid is still remembered as a remarkable feat of precision bombing. Unfortunately, Gibson's faithful pet Labrador, Nigger is not remembered for his loyalty in quite the same way, since his name is now considered to be offensive to certain members of society, not our dark skinned cousins but the politically correct bunch of interfering twats in Westminster and Brussels. Thus when it came to remaking the film of the raids, the Americans did what they do best, they rewrote history and renamed the poor canine Digger, in a similar way that they introduced a digger into the remake of Robin Hood and gave the cast of Braveheart Australian accents.

Unfortunately, world markets had not been kind to either company, and in the early eighties both factories closed their doors for the last time, thus removing, within a short time frame, the towns major sources of employment, a blow from which it has taken the town twenty five years to recover. Market forces had succeeded where Hitler had miserably failed, only recently, with European and private funding, have the derelict warehouses, maltings and factories along the riverbanks been converted to luxury apartments and homes. Britannia works, once one of the largest boiler making facilities in Europe is now being converted into 'Marshall's Yard' a forty million pound retail development, which no doubt will be identical to every other soulless £40 million shopping complex and will belittle the skills of the men who toiled and sweated on the site for the best part of a century, such is progress.

Gainsborough had not fared well from the loss of it's manufacturing base, it had become rundown and tired, as a friend of mine so eloquently stated 'Gainsborough smelt of hot cornflakes or shit' depending on which way the wind was blowing, the first statement was a reference to the aroma which emanated from the local maltings, the second was self explanatory, it did however have a loyal community who tended to remain put, like rats in a sewer, and soldier on in the face of adversity. On my first visit I formed the opinion that the locals were thirty years behind the times, some of them still believed that the world was flat, many of them never dared to cross the bridge over the Trent to Nottinghamshire for fear of falling off the edge of the world, although a few of them had heard of the fabled nirvana of Doncaster some twenty miles away. This opinion was in no way ameliorated when I observed that the residents still pointed excitedly at passing planes with jaws agape and an expression of awe, more worryingly they insisted on throwing bread to passing helicopters. I became aware that Gainsborough was different from other towns when, on my first visit, I noticed the home made banner, hurriedly fashioned from an old bed sheet, hanging from an upstairs window in a row of terraced houses. On it were proudly printed the words 'Happy 30th birthday Grandma', it was that sort of town, where everybody knew everyone else, sometimes a little too intimately. My formative impressions were only strengthened when I visited the local recycle station, where I was confronted with an extra receptacle for used syringes and the locals were making withdrawals from the clothes bank. I have since discovered during my enforced internments in the town ,that even the birds that reside in Gainsborough are not quite normal, unlike their rural counterparts in the rest of Britain, they remain silent throughout the day and then proceed to serenade the locals throughout the night as though possessed by some variant form of avian Tourette's, I have since realised that like most of the inhabitants of the town, the birds are possibly too frightened to venture out during daylight hours for fear of being mugged or worst still contracting the bizarre genetic disorder which warps reasoning and convinces those infected that the town is no different to any other and that everybody sleeps with their grandmother at some point in their life. When I mentioned this phenomenon to one of the brighter residents he postulated that the birds must have being Nightingales, even when I explained that if that were true the locals would have either eaten them or sold them in order to fund drug habits long ago and that his theory would also suggest that Gainsborough was host

14

to the largest population of Nightingales on the planet , he remained unconvinced and promptly left in search of his copy of the observer's book of birds, in order to further his theory, I can only assume that his version had been printed in block capitals and large print format ,with the added bonus of picture clues. Whilst it is undoubtedly true to say that Gainsborough is home to some of the commonest 'birds' in the country, Luscinia Megarhynchos is most certainly not amongst them!

The town apparently experienced a brief moment of fame in the latter part of the twentieth century when the son of a local gypsy family was eaten by a lion, honestly, you could not make this shit up. The renowned Robert brothers circus was performing in the town and the animals, including the lions, as per usual, were in their cages on site, the young man by the name of Jackson-Parr, decided that hours of fun could be had by taunting the lions and promptly provided them with an all too intimate pyrotechnic display with the help of some particularly loud bangers, the lions, similarly, decided that even more fun could be had by escaping from their enclosure in shear panic and promptly ripped the precious little low life to bits, before dragging his remains up a handy nearby tree and partially devouring the juicy bits. According to Clarence, the sub species tastes a little like human with just a hint of hedgehog, he also expressed a preference for having them baked in mud over an open fire, apparently, this form of cuisine aids in the removal of spines and unwanted hairs. Sadly the unfortunate and innocent animal had to be destroyed since the authorities believed that it may have contracted various unpleasant and incurable diseases during its ordeal, presumably the moral of the tale is 'do not fuck about with large carnivorous animals and fireworks', at the very least it could end up costing you an arm and a leg. On a more serious note, a gentleman by the name of Hall, received bruising to his head when the kangaroo, which also escaped as a result of the melee, jumped over the bonnet of a car on which he was working at the time, closely pursued by its keepers, as the newly liberated animal endeavoured to take in the bright lights of Gainsborough.

Gainsborough did however have a couple of gems hidden away, firstly it had the Old Hall a 15th century timbered manor house founded by Thomas Burgh with a magnificent brick kitchen and great hall, during it's lifetime it had played host to King Richard III and Henry VIII, now it's grounds play host to drug addicts and teenagers drinking super strength cider. Secondly, Gainsborough was home of the Queen Elizabeth Grammar school, this was my raison d'être. The school had an impressive educational record and was rated as one of the best in the country. In order that my son would received the best possible education I had taken it upon myself to secure a place for him. This was not an easy task, in truth it would have been easier to plait the fog that rolled off the river Trent on a winter's morning. The schools annual intake of pupils was 180, because of it's reputation this figure was always massively oversubscribed, thus places were allocated by various criteria, one of which was the family residences proximity to the school. To cut a long story short, after a visit to the local estate agent, I bought the nearest house to the school gates, my son was the 180th pupil accepted, much to my relief, at least my son would receive a good education, or so I thought. At this juncture I could not possibly have known that my little angel's major qualifications on leaving school would be a worrying knowledge of the price and availability of certain pharmaceuticals, the ability to hot wire a Fiesta in under two minutes and the agility to wrap a larger than average Jamaican woodbine with one hand, he also had a less than healthy knowledge of the anatomy and physiology of the opposite sex and had developed an uncanny ability in marketing which made Arthur Daley and Del Trotter look like rank amateurs, to make matters worse he had decided to mimic the sleeping patterns of his pet hamster and spent most of his day studying the inside of his eyelids (his own not the hamsters that is) similarly his toilet habits and personal hygiene were hardly more advanced. I had endeavoured to tempt him into the real world with various incentives, all to no avail, when bribery and extreme violence also failed to stir him from his nocturnal fantasy world, I decided the only solution would be to employ him in the pub, quite as what I had no idea, since, I had seen more life on the cat's back and more work in a giro. Throughout the testing times of juniors adolescence and despite his less than eager attempts to gain an education, I had consoled myself with two thoughts, firstly, I would not have to make the long drive to London to witness my son embarrass himself in an episode of University Challenge by having his educational deficiencies exposed at the hands of Jeremy Tampax and co, and secondly, if my family had not moved to Gainsborough, I would not be the proud owner of a fine hostelry revered by many disciples of the hop and barley persuasion, which thanks to the towns revival had drastically increased in value and thus was probably the most prudent investment I would ever make.

The Eight Jolly Brewers, whilst being something of an oxymoron, was and still is, a one off. It is a village pub in the centre of town, in the mornings the bar resembled a cross between God's waiting room and the restaurant at the end of the universe. The older residents would while away the hours shouting at each other and drinking, some because they had forgotten to turn on their hearing aids, others who just liked shouting for shouting's sake, some quietly read the papers and picked out the days winners or gazed at the numerous beer mats which adorned the walls and ceilings, whilst savouring the cellars secrets, others just sat and pissed themselves, for once I mean literally not metaphorically. At lunchtimes the suits would arrive, solicitors, accountants, judges, council high fliers all resplendent in Mr Burton's finest with an overwhelming ambition to talk about football, rugby and cricket and discuss how and why England's finest teams had once again failed to qualify or had been comprehensively beaten by some 3rd world country. How they thought they could solve that enigma in the space of a one hour lunch break was a constant source of wonder to my simple brain, after all I knew two things about sport, nothing and fuck all!.

The evenings brought a different throng of thirsty disciples from a wide hinterland, like moths to a flame they came on their pilgrimage to sample the elixir of the barley, the pub was like Lourdes, with proper toilets, but without the miracles. I had repeatedly tried to find a crying virgin but had failed miserably, I later learned that in Gainsborough the literal definition of a virgin was someone who could outrun their father and brother not to mention the family pit-bull.

Another bonus of owning the pub was that I regularly got to meet the performers from the local jazz club, which was situated some two hundred yards away. It was not unusual for the bar to be full of the BBC jazz orchestra and stalwarts of the genre such as George Melly, Kenny Ball and Cleo Laine and friends. Initially, owning the pub was good fun, the hours and days flew by, it was a welcome distraction from being a husband and a father, there was also a certain satisfaction to be had from seeing customers, who had slightly over indulged in the pleasures of the glass, stumble out of the door at closing time with a grotesque rhinocerpig of a women, who would probably have made a better truffle hunter in the south of France than a bed partner, believing that they had pulled Aby Titmuss's twin sister. Sometimes it was a blessing that the Norwegian whaling fleet no longer anchored in the Trent, for they would have soon depleted their harpoon stores and the ensuing glut would have caused the world price of whale oil to rapidly plummet.

Eventually, however, the novelty of owning a pub began to wane, despite the fact that I had diversified my business interests and bought a small brewery, I was becoming tired of beer and its effects on my customers. I never quite managed to enter their surreal worlds, apparently I didn't have the requisite **visa,** some of them spent more time in the pub than I did, Some even had their mail delivered there, sometimes I expected them to pay for drinks in 'Varks' rather than the coin of the realm, in reality it was more likely to be a giro which was the coin of this particular realm. The stress was beginning to show, I was becoming less and less tolerant and was relying more and more on my staff. I kept out of the way as much as possible to the point where I made Howard Hughes look like a socialite, my marriage was beginning to crumble and the efforts of juniors wayward antics were hitting home.

It was round about this time that I formulated my 98% rule, which basically stated that 98% of the population were in some way retarded and hard of learning. This was based on the gathering of sound scientific data observed from behind the bar over a four year period, in many bars in the UK the figure was nearer to 100%, in a select few around Cambridge it was nearer 97.5%, although I never empirically proved the theory, I had collected sufficient evidence to substantiate my beliefs.

Take for example the young 'lady' customer who was convinced that the East Yorkshire city of Hull, was in fact situated abroad, perhaps she knew something about plate tectonics of which I was not aware, and the region had moved significantly overnight, or perhaps she was just plain fucking simple. Informing her that the world's longest single span suspension bridge only served to connect the lesser mortals on the south side of the Humber with those north of the river did precious little to convince said simpleton, who could not, it seemed, conceive that Hull was in fact connected to the rest of the mainland without recourse to concrete and steel, and that the small buildings upon the bridge were actually toll booths and not, as she had presumed, passport control. Furthermore her assertion that mussels came from parts of a fish and were not in fact bivalve molluscs, did little to bolster her respect and standing in the pub community, which fish and from what parts was never adequately explained and to this day remains an enduring enigma. Unsurprisingly before the end of her teenage years the lady in question had miraculously found the correct technique and aperture and reproduced, she also succeeded in getting herself married, although the marriage only lasted for a month, which was by all accounts marginally longer than the dowry and presents did. Magically, the wedding present from the local authority was a nice new house, duly furnished in the appropriate manner, with unfeasibly large plasma TV, the accommodation afforded her the luxury of living on Pringles and chocolate cake, it seemed that the lady's idea of a balanced diet was a little of each in both hands .In short the girl, for that was what she was, was a walking two legged microcosm of all that is wrong with Team GB, my belief that she had in fact been written by the great fictional philanthropist Jeremy Kyle, and was not in fact anywhere approaching real, did not meet with a warm response from either her or her family. It seemed highly likely that thanks to Britain's watered down education system, this lady would probably go on to become a research scientist for Homebase or one of those annoying bastards who invent toasters which neither toast bread correctly or have slots large enough to accept an average sized piece of bread, and are in short about as useful as a fart in a wind tunnel.

A further example of the educational oasis of mediocrity in a desert of social ignorance that is Gainsborough, was graphically demonstrated by the twenty stone something, replete with the requisite number of tattoos, piercings and gluteal biscuit shelf who, in a break with local traditions and protocol, ordered a chicken and bacon salad for one of her lunches. One can only assume that the kitchen had run out of chicken nuggets and burgers, and that the lady fancied a touch of the exotic in a thinly veiled attempt to impress her friends, in truth she had probably learned of the fabled dish from an episode of 'Come dine with me', for sure, judging by her appearance she had not actually seen a salad before except in the glossy pages of a magazine whilst waiting for the dole office to open on a Monday morning. Following delivery of her meal to her table, the lady beckoned the waiter and via a string of expletives and misplaced adjectives, which would have made a coal miner blush, if obviously, they had not become an extinct subspecies and disappeared long ago, explained that she had not ordered 'any fucking mushy peas with her frigging salad' and requested that he should return the meal to the kitchen and insert it in to the chef via the outbound aperture, whereupon the fountain of knowledge and lard was quietly informed that the small green pile on her plate was not of leguminous origin but was in fact Guacamole whose ancestry was more closely related to the humble avocado, perhaps it was the excitement of seeing her first salad which confused her diminutive brain, whose size was in no way commensurate with the size of her arse. The ladies social standing and respect took a further rapid shift in a downward direction, when she announced to the small, equally ignorant congregation gathered around her table, that 'she did not keep a horse and bark herself', presumably she whiled away her schooldays scoffing crisps and dripping sandwiches rather than attending biology classes, obviously this assertion assumes that the retard in question did actually attend a place of education somewhere in her very dim and distant past, which on reflection seems about as feasible as her not getting arseholed on a Friday night on vodka shots and lager before depositing the aforementioned salad in some poor unfortunate's doorway in the shape of a pavement pizza. To cite the words of Gainsborough's first surviving brain donor, and chairman of the local branch of the Lincolnshire lobotomy society, 'if my father had been alive today, he would be turning in his grave'.

The gent's toilets were another case worthy of closer scrutiny. When I first bought the pub the first thing I did was refurbish the toilets at great personal expense of both time and money, not to mention hard work. The toilets had been neglected for many years, they were dirty and smelt like some of my less sanitary customers. I had single handedly ripped up many layers of vinyl flooring with my bare hands, which, since they had been soaking up recycled beer and snot for some fifteen years, was not the most pleasant of chores, although surprisingly memorable, the floor resembled a veritable piss sandwich ,and meant that I had to toil long hours throughout the nights to bring a degree of cleanliness and hygiene to my establishment. Many people rightly judge the cleanliness of a hostelry by the standard of it's toilets, this is especially true of the ladies. Understandable then that I should get a little miffed when people abused my tour de force. I could understand the thieving, after all this was Gainsborough where felony was almost compulsory and was still taught to A level standard in the local schools, thus, over time, the toilet rolls, soap, and even the ash trays all disappeared. The latter had become an ongoing battle, each time that they were stolen I would replace them with another, gradually the replacements became older and more decrepit in a futile attempt to deter the would be felons. I wondered how dirty their homes must have been that they would want to furnish their coffee tables with a broken and filthy Timothy Taylors ashtray as a trophy from Friday nights debauched session with Aby's sister. In a final attempt to smash the ashtray dealing ring, I replaced them with peanut tins, empty of course, this provided the inmates with a new and interesting challenge, these too were stolen or used instead of the urinal, quite why eluded me totally, the urinal was 8 foot long, the tin was 3 inches in diameter, the older customers just pissed on the floor in the in the time honoured manner. Not to be outdone, I pierced the replacement tins with a series of holes, this time it would be their trousers and feet which were the recipients of the contents of their bladders and not my ashtrays. The theft of the electronic air fresheners was a little harder to comprehend since they were seven feet up the wall and securely screwed to it, or so I thought. This theft was only mildly overshadowed by the loss of an 8 foot fluorescent light tube, how did they remove it from the ceiling in the first place? And how did they smuggle an 8 foot light through the busy pub? Both of these bizarre crimes against mentality were however eclipsed when the 240 volt electronic hand drier went westwards, it was at this point that I considered the introduction of passport control for the toilets. I even considered locking the toilets so that the inmates would have to piss in the car park as was customary with the patrons of the surrounding bars. This was a direct result of their facilities being located upstairs, since they did not contain ashtrays and the physical exertion was presumably too stressful for their inactive clientele, the long walk to their conveniences was seldom undertaken, as mentioned , they preferred to use the car park en-route to the next venue. It was apparent that Gainsborough's gene pool was in need of the addition of a large amount of chlorine. I determined that, God forbid , I should ever be unfortunate enough to have a sudden attack of public spiritedness, I would pay to install a series of road signs on the entry roads to the town duly proclaiming "Please kill our children, not your speed", with an addendum requesting that the driver should reverse for a second attempt at compassionate euthanasia in order to target the victim's second head and assist in the eradication of the widespread inbreeding and genetic aberrations which were endemic to the region.

If the articles which my customers removed from the toilets seemed bizarre, the ones left behind were even more intriguing. The coat hangers and various items of clothing were at first puzzling, until I discovered this was due to the local shoplifters who were usually 'smacked off their heads' thanks to Charlie, Harry, Fred or whatever other substance was available at the time. They would run into the toilets and rapidly change attire for ones they had stolen from the surrounding shops, in an attempt to evade the long arm of the law. As I have already pointed out, they need not have worried, they had ample time to spin the yarn and hand knit a new garment before plod sauntered up, quite why they found it necessary to leave their underpants, I have no idea. The empty condom packets and the 'Anne Summers purple electronic vibrating knob ring' deposited in the gents were a little more difficult to comprehend, I mean purple for God's sake, what was it's owner thinking of, the evening dress and stilettos have still evaded explanation. Then there were the articles which customers deposited down the toilets, where do men think fag packets and second hand chewing gum are going to go when they casually throw them in the urinals? Surely it is not only the inhabitants of Gainsborough who piss in ashtrays and put their cigarettes out in urinals. On one occasion a lady customer informed my manager that there were flowers in the ladies toilets. "I know" he replied, "they've been there for ages", after several attempts to explain herself, each one more insistent than the last, he realised what she meant. The two vases of dried flowers which normally adorned the wash basins had been thrown into the toilet bowls, one per toilet complete with their contents, how much more proof of my 98% rule do you require? At least the air freshener was still there.

The previous owner of the pub had learned his trade in Hull, over a beer one night he related a story which made my tales of conveniences seem almost tame. Apparently on discovering a blockage in the ladies toilet, which necessitated the use of an arm around the u-bend, he believed that he could feel the body of a baby. Believing that a customer had aborted her pregnancy whilst on his premises, he contacted the local police, who after the requisite period of waiting, duly arrived and removed the carcass of a frozen chicken, how much more proof do you need? I could not make these stories up, in the pub game, fact is definitely stranger than fiction.

The loss of various pieces of my property I could deal with, but there was one customer in particular whose toilet antics really pushed my patience to the limit. The anally retentive throwback in question had decided that he did not like the virginal whiteness of the pristine ceramic tiles which now adorned the gents toilet walls, and the voices in his head had apparently instructed him to smear the contents of his nasal passages all over their surface. This somewhat less then hygienic hobby continued for weeks, such were the adhesive properties of his nose scabs that if he had sold the formula to a superglue manufacturing firm he would never have had to work again, not that he ever did, sometimes it was almost necessary to remove the residue with a chisel or an angle grinder! What in Gods name drives the amoeboid brain cells of people like this? I could picture the halfwit as a child, sat on his front door step, diligently picking away, up to his knuckles in work; flicking the odd carefully rolled missile at the cat. For certain he had not acquired his adeptness at nasal husbandry over night, this ability had matured from an early age, perhaps encouraged by his fathers and his grandfathers who had carefully groomed him in the green art. No, he was the prodigy of a long line of finger farmers, he was the last exponent of the nose artisans trade, of that I was going to make certain, at least while he was on my premises. I duly typed the notice below and placed it in the gents, (SEE LETTER) it very rapidly had the desired effect and, since then, the tiles have remained unsullied. I think it was the threat of DNA testing that frightened him the most, he need not have worried, no database in the world would have found a match, his mitochondrial mush was an amalgam of slug and cabbage.

Sometimes, in Gainsborough, it is not difficult to envisage that man in some primordial past crawled out of the swamp, started to breath air and walk in an upright manner, what is a little more cerebrally taxing is the fact that the species has survived for this long. If you look closely at some of the inhabitants of Gainsborough it is still possible to detect the vestiges of gills, and some of the residents still walk on all fours, especially on Friday and Saturday nights.

By this stage in my career as a landlord, it had become very apparent that I would have more chance of glimpsing a naked Lord Lucan riding Shergar through the market square in Gainsborough on a busy Saturday morning, than understanding the actions of some of my patrons. Sure, the antics of the nose farmer were bizarre and socially unacceptable but, in truth, his behaviour was no doubt normal for him, he wasn't quite a full vark and it seemed to me that he had a few sandwiches missing from his lunchbox, although he would have to work harder if he was to become a fully qualified window licker, so his bodily misdemeanours I could just about forgive.

One of my elderly customers was unfortunate enough to require the use of a colostomy bag, which, whilst for him, it was a 'pain in the arse', or not as the case may have been, it did at least keep him warm on a cold winter's morning. From time to time, fuelled by an excessive and over exuberant filling via a pint pot, the receptacle would explode, as the saying goes 'the shit would hit the fan'. Fortunately by this time it's owner had usually completed the journey to the gents, but the subsequent fallout would take more than a little cleaning up, still, he was amongst friends and, in his case, it was always an accident, again this was forgivable and part of the joys of being a landlord, or as was more usually the case, the joys of being a manager or lower minion, such is the art of delegation.

The shit smearer was a different ball game altogether. This customer, it would seem, dined on an explosive cocktail of Semtex and duck eggs, washed down with copious amounts of the amber nectar and syrup of figs, before depositing the resultant residue in a most acrobatic display, it was less the result of Epsom salts more the product of somersaults, the ensuing filth and destruction appeared as though a flock of dare devil seagulls piloted by wing commander Guy Gibson and the Dambusters had swooped on the toilet pan, seat, floor or anything else within a worryingly wide area in a daring airborne assault. Could it be possible that scientists had successfully artificially inseminated his mother with the genes of a lawn sprinkler? As if the initial part of the operation was not stomach churning enough, his attempts at cleaning himself were even more flawed, it was inevitable that the toilet rolls would become encrusted with more than a scant coating of shit inside the cardboard tube, even the spare roll on the window sill, some four feet up the wall did not escape his faecal violations, quite how, I could only begin to imagine. This was not a one off occurrence, it happened with worrying regularity, the problem was how I should approach the subject? It was hardly feasible to walk up to the customer on a Sunday lunch time and utter the words, 'excuse me sir but would you please desist from smearing your shit all over my premises', even I wasn't that forthright. One thing was certain, I would no longer shake the hand of the customer in question. Strangely, the man, in question had chosen a career in printing as a way of paying his bills, this was an unusual choice since he was acutely dyslexic, borderline thick, and found it impossible to construct a sentence or use grammar correctly. This was perhaps the reason why his parents had given him a name which only consisted of three letters, I assumed that they had figured that, via the law of averages, even he had a reasonable chance of spelling his name correctly on his benefit applications. Bizarrely, his wife's sanitary manners were no better, since she apparently considered it normal procedure to shit in the 'sanni' bins in the ladies toilet rather than the more accepted method of depositing one's breakfast down the porcelain receptacle provided.For many years both herself and her husband were kept in toilet tissue and liquid soap by my good self, since neither one thought anything of stealing as much of either commodity as was possible at any opportunity, during their depraved toilet sojourns. I can only assume that the lady's behaviour was the result of a drunken visit to Greece where the whole ablution thing is somewhat different, her confusion obviously resulted in her shitting in the bin and throwing the paper down the bog instead of vice versa, either way the episode left a bad feeling not to mention a bad smell.

The grey haired septuagenarian who presented himself at the bar on market days was, to say the least, a little enigmatic, in truth he was something of a maverick of his generation. He would buy a tomato juice and then proceed to stand for ages staring at the pictures which hung on the walls, it appeared that his favourite pictures adorned the upstairs rooms, these rooms were rarely used by anybody else during the week. In my naivety I assumed that he preferred his own company and the solitude, probably reflecting on days gone by, past loves and friends long gone, however, it was not long before the true reason for his self imposed exile to the darker corners of the building became apparent. Following a visit from our local plumber, who had been duly summoned to fix a malfunctioning gents toilet, it was discovered that the fault was the result of a part empty bottle of Polish vodka having been inserted into the cistern, it appeared that on his frequent and lengthy visits, to the toilet, dutifully accompanied by his tomato juice, the dear old elderly bastard was secretly topping up his innocuous drink with fifty per cent proof. Furthermore ,the old campaigner had taken, a little too regularly it would seem, to 'shaking hands with the unemployed,' as it were, whilst ensconced in his den of depravity, if he had had the foresight to avail himself of the services of a pedometer strapped to his wrist he could quite easily have knocked up a good few miles before lunch, such was the vigour with which he approached his antisocial indulgence. His popularity ratings sank even further when the local Tesco store manager informed me that the gentleman in question was barred from his store for what can best be described as crimes against decency and hygiene involving his trouser apparel and his right hand, whilst perusing the food aisle ,who says men cannot multitask? The assertion was endorsed shortly after this revelation when granddad filth was caught 'red handed', in the most literal sense of the word, repeating his acclaimed performance in the gent's with his trousers at half mast and a roll of Andrex in his left hand ,what he was doing with his right hand is perhaps better left to the imagination. Needless to say he was hurriedly despatched through the door and told not to return , for fear that his affliction was contagious. I assume that he probably now whiles away the hours at the local Salvation Army cocktail bar cutting cocaine with his bus pass whilst watching 'BabeStation' on Freeview. Once again this incident underlines the inherent dangers involved in shaking hands with customers in public houses, but at least shows that with the appropriate training it is still possible to be a wanker well after reaching retirement age; and to think that in my naivety I thought that the calluses on his hands were the result of years of hard graft!

By now my job satisfaction figures were lower than a Basset hounds bollocks and a strangely diminutive Basset hound with incredibly short legs at that, if this trend continued the dog in question would require the immediate fitting of a sump guard around its southernmost parts.

Despite the Neanderthal actions of some customers, there were many genuine people in Gainsborough who were the salt of the earth. Over the years these people became good friends, especially the older regulars who's manners and morals were impeccable. Elmer had been a glider pilot at Arnhem and was about as stubborn as it was possible to be without enrolling on a lengthy course of advanced stubbornness or being a stain on the pub wanker's Y-fronts.Following a fall, it took Elmer a good half an hour to walk the 300 yards from his home to the pub, his progress was painful to observe, even with the assistance of his walking frame, whose approach could be heard long before it's owner arrived ,as it's metal legs were eroded week by week by the pavement's surface, if he had survived a few more weeks he would have had to replace it or crawl to his destination on all fours with a severely shortened design. Typical of his generation, and sadly absent from today's, his determination and resolve were inspirational, rather than seek help he would soldier on, and woe betide anybody or anything who had the affront to get in his way, such a proud veteran of life's campaign, albeit a cantankerous old bastard. He would not allow anyone to buy him a drink, charity was taboo and a last resort for his generation, with me he didn't have a choice, I would buy him a drink and he would open up his heart and produce photographs from his well worn wallet and relate stories of his past life, traversed with his harrowing experiences of war and hardships, which I struggled even to begin to understand. Another proud national ambassador was Mr Hill, he too had served his country through wartime in the Royal Fleet Arm and the Merchant Navy, he would recount similar stories of hardships and bravery, I can still picture his frail and emaciated frame before he died, another victim of the evil that is cancer, what the might of the German army failed to do a few malignant cells accomplished almost overnight. Drew was another perfect gentleman, who in later years had helped to restore church organs, a finer man never walked the planet, I can still hear his mellow dulcet voice, all these men sadly are no longer with us but their memories are indelibly etched in time. Bill however is still going strong, he loves his beer, sport and music, he once had the misfortune of booking the same holiday as myself to Tenerife, poor sod, and for all his advancing years was great company. Men like this built Gainsborough,being in their company was one of the few bonuses of owning a public house. Others were characters like Billy the Hatchet, he had been brought up in Glasgow in hard times, he was revered as one of the best safe breakers around, quite which college he attended to learn his skills I never discovered. He would relate tales of filtering Brasso through a pair of stockings, in order to obtain a drink, or of selling bottles of cold tea and passing them off as whisky on Glasgow's back streets and tenement blocks, if possible Billy would skin a fart, and no doubt sell the skin. His doctor had informed him that he was drinking too much beer and whisky, which was causing his health to deteriorate, the doctor's recommendation, which Billy took a little too literally, was that he should try a glass or two of red wine instead. Billy took this to mean he should drink at least two litres a day, after several close encounters with the pavements and lamp posts on the way home, Billy suffered a stroke and sadly died, some months later, a shadow of his former roguish self. My enduring memory of Billy was formed one night over a few drinks, When I asked him if he would fight for the honour of my friends new wife, to which Billy replied, in an accent that crossed the Lincolnshire, Scottish borders, "no but I'd fight to get on her", such was Billy's sense of humour, characters like him along with the moral fabric of modern life, seem to be rapidly disappearing.

Many local hostelries supported football and cricket teams or pool and darts leagues, since most of our customers were either, disabled in some manner or were somewhat depleted in the limb   number/operational   effectiveness department, too old, or just plain, too fucking idle to participate in such frivolous activities, preferring as they did to while away their leisure hours, of which they apparently had an abundance, rolling fags, necking copious amounts of falling down juice and shouting at each other incoherently, The Eight Jolly Brewers did not indulge in any such flagrant wastes of drinking time or energy. On reflection, given the primitive nature of some customers and the defective eyesight of others, it did not seem appropriate to arm the clientele with lethal weapons of a sharp pointy nature i.e. darts or pool cues. Instead the hours were passed, or dragged depending on one's standpoint/brain capacity, in team activities of a more sedate, unusual and wholly inappropriate manner. For example, one particular customer who shall remain nameless; although this prudence seems somewhat futile, since Gainsborough is not to the best of my knowledge exactly awash with one legged Lolly-Pop men called Brian, was the subject of one such bizarre pub activity. Nameless Brian had the sort of face which suggested he could well have been the love child of Stan of Coronation Street fame, this theory was only compounded by the fact that the two men also shared the same surname, to say that he was photogenic would have been stretching the point by quite a large factor, rather he had a face like a Pit-bull chewing a wasp. Brian was unfortunate enough to have propagated an impressive collection of gangrene and putrefying bacteria colonies on his foot, this gave rise to the interactive team pastime of watching Brian's lower limb rot and placing side bets on the infection's weekly advancement whilst quaffing a few pints and discussing the weather and other such trivia. Whilst, in truth, I do not envisage a national interactive rotting limb league being established at any time in the near future, I have had the prudence and foresight to copyright the name and television coverage. Eventually, the infection won the second Battle of Wounded Knee and Brian had to have the lower section of his leg amputated, at least we assume that he did since the next time we saw him he no longer had the stinking rotten appendage but did have a neatly bandaged stump and a spare shoe, these facts gave credence to the fact that he had not simply been careless and misplaced his leg but had in fact had it surgically removed. The fact that Brian was now one leg short in the number of legs department not only meant that he no longer needed to buy shoes, since he was able to nick the solitary display item from outside Timpson's, if he remembered to swipe the correct foot, which for Brian was possibly pushing the boundaries somewhat, but his loss also gave rise to yet another interactive pub game. Whilst kicking the cripples false leg or twatting it with his walking stick in an attempt to shock or anger any new and hence unaware disciples to the licensed sanatorium, inevitably elicited fits of laughter, the game became a whole lot more interesting after a few sherbets when it became far more difficult to remember which was the real and which was the false leg, oh how we chortled when we got it wrong, sick bastards every last one. Since the other wizard wheeze to be had on Brian's expense tab was to surreptitiously free the safety catch on his newly acquired walking stick which inevitably would lead to some pretty impressive acrobatics for an ageing one legged old fart when he attempted to put any weight on to the useless support, his shortage of limbs and defective aids meant that it was a miracle that the poor man ever walked again and made the exceptional recovery that he did.

Another bonus of being the custodian of my temple of fun, was being able to listen to some great live music on Thursday nights. I had called in favours from musical colleagues and established a good reputation for various types of music. This gave me an even greater satisfaction since I had dispatched the local folk club, which used to meet in the pub on a Friday night, to the Coventry Arms, or whatever its name was. The Brewers had become a regular meet of bearded recluses, teachers and social workers, most of them wearing Arran sweaters and sandals and with a strange profusion of ear lobe hairs, many of them, I am certain, were professional tree huggers. they had mastered the technique of walking around with one finger lodged firmly in an ear whilst chanting 'Hey Nonny Nonny' and were adept at making one orange cordial last a week. Heaven help any unsuspecting customer who spoke, or farted, at an ill considered time, any customer smoking would meet with the same derision. I used to do all three, just to piss them off, especially the teachers, I had developed a healthy disrespect for these exonerated elite who seemed to think that they could conduct their everyday lives as though they were still in the classroom, terrorising their five year old pupils. Over the years, I had formed the opinion that since it was now only necessary to place a cross in the correct place on an examination paper to receive a grade A GCSE in advanced thermodynamics and applied masturbation in the third world, or other such equally diverse and obscure topic which would have absolutely no relevance to the real world, the academic quality of the education system's output had gradually deteriorated. Thus the following intake into higher education and ultimately teacher training, suffered a similar decline, with each successive year being dimmer than the last. It seemed that education was on a dangerous downward spiral which would ultimately end in disaster and necessitate that future pupils would need to speak Chinese if they were to have any chance of finding a job. In part I blamed the system for my son's spectacular failings at school, it seemed that the tutors lived in a fluffy, cotton wool world where pupils did not indulge in pleasures of the flesh or the bottle and the worst crimes they could commit were scrumping apples or dropping itching powder down a fellow pupils shirt, before diligently settling down to do their homework, heaven forbid they could even spell the word amphetamine. How I would dearly love to sit them down in the town centre on a Friday night and show them the real world most people live in. I had become a disciple of the tenet 'those who can, do, those who can't, teach' long gone were the teachers of my formative years where respect was paramount, they had been replaced with a bunch of arrogant oxygen scavengers who lived in a different world to myself.

During a folk club meeting on Friday night, one particular female teacher, I use the term loosely on both counts, became progressively more irate since I refused to allow her to charge my regular customers a three pound entrance fee for the evening's entertainment, I pointed out that I owned the place and I would make the rules, before politely enquiring if she had considered seeking relief from her problem via the use of hormone patches or holistic medicines. At this point one of her colleagues, no doubt a fellow blackboard rubber throwing bully, informed me that I could not speak to the wizened old bitch in such a manner; why do people in Gainsborough insist on telling me this one liner?, was he a friend of PC Dim perhaps. Following his interjection, I enlightened him with the news, "yes I can, I own the place, now fuck off the lot of you," Kofie Annan would have been proud of me. The welcome spring sunshine teemed through the open front doors of the pub it's warm glow filled the bar, it was customary at this time of year to have the doors to 'the olive grove', as old Drew had christened the seasonal portal to Hades, open to the elements, this allowed the inmates unrestricted views of the wonders of Gainsborough. A small coven of friends and customers had gathered by an adjacent table and were enjoying the morning's first oesophageal embrocations of the house, whilst discussing the relative importance of the day's news, state of the country and the size of the tits, arse or thighs of any female unfortunate enough to traverse the doorway. As far as I can recall nobody ever enquired as to why Big Stef was so called, even to a one eyed myopic retard on controlled drugs, who was having a bad day, a commodity which Gainsborough produced in droves, would have had a fair suspicion as to the origins of the moniker.

Stef was a thickset, swarthy looking thirty something with a shock of unkempt hair which the international hair beauty product suppliers had long since given up on. He was a quietly spoken proverbial brick shithouse, with which, pride and a modicum of self preservation dictated that it would be foolhardy in the extreme to mess around with, or his wife too for that matter, it was acknowledged throughout the town that if there was trouble it would, likely as not, be the big man who would bring it to a premature conclusion, in all probability this would involve the perpetrators partaking of an unscheduled siesta on the nearest floor, minus a number of teeth, bones and/or ears, the man's reach and punch were the stories of local folklore and were considered to be far longer than his tolerance of muppets. The truth was that he was better known for these attributes than his patience or conciliatory abilities, the man apparently ate coiled springs for breakfast washed down with lashings of Irish whiskey.

The dishevelled unshaven tramp stumbled through the doors of the olive grove several seconds after the overpowering aroma of shit, body odour and alcohol, all of which, it seemed, had been prematurely ejected from his person via various outlets, if the signs were to be believed at any rate, the two six inch snot candles which festooned his nostrils on their inevitable path to his lips, stood testament to the man's inebriation and disregard for any vestige of personal hygiene. He turned to Stef and fixedly stared into the back of his head, his eyes preoccupied whilst the rest of his body rocked and swayed like a demented owl with Parkinson's. 'Hey fatboy', he blurted, through a curtain of saliva/alcohol, in Stef's general direction, 'last night I fucked your mother, the dirty cow was gagging for it, fair turned her inside out I did, the dirty cow. The dog did her from behind whilst she sucked my cock for half the night, she finished up sore as fuck and had a face like a plasterer's trowel'. The cockroaches had, by this point in the conversation, long stopped farting and were intently listening to the drunken idiot with the suicide wish's interjection, even the pins had ceased falling, the assembled throng, meanwhile, were slowly edging away from the epicentre of the forthcoming Armageddon which was surely about to unfold before them. By the time the nutter had got as far as 'Hey fatboy', it was obvious that he had won first prize in the 'you're going for an early sleep via the application of extreme violence and knuckle anaesthetic contest. Surprisingly, the big man barely moved, the obligatory red mist which usually bellowed from his facial apertures, at such times, was patently absent, instead, he threw the remnants of his whiskey down the back of his throat, glanced around his worried congregation, which by this point in proceedings were clearly expecting a bloodbath, if not the weeks first murder, and duly enquired 'same again lads', before approaching the swaying drunk, who it seemed was still defying all that Isaac Newton held dear together with his lifetime's works inherent inconveniences, he gently raised his hands onto his shoulders and respectfully said 'Dad you're pissed again, you can have a coke and then you're going home. What was even more surprising to those gathered therein than the lack of violence, was the fact that Stef was apparently born of woman and was not the result of some errant Shelly like laboratory experiment which at some point had gone horribly awry.

The Eight Jolly Brewers had a reputation for great beers from around the country as well as numerous bottled beers from Germany, Belgium,

Holland, Poland and the Czech Republic. One of the benefits of being the owner was that two dozen beers on stillage had to be tested everyday. This was not the pasteurised branded keg beer which was constantly rammed down our throats by the big boys of the brewing world, this was a lovingly crafted living product which needed to be cosseted and cajoled into pristine condition, each beer had it's own characteristics, the customers knew their beers and rightly demanded , and received, a quality drink, whether is was an ale, mild, porter, stout or lager.

Some of the beers on offer were brewed by my own brewery located in a small village named Wellow in Nottinghamshire. The village was noted for being the home of the tallest maypole in the country, hence the brewery was called 'Maypole Brewery Ltd', it wasn't an inspired name but it worked. Similarly, the beers it produced had unimaginative names, since most began with the word May. Maybee was infused with local honey, Mayhem did what it said on the tin, since it was a strong dark ale, Mayfair, Mae West, May Day Mild and Wonkey Donkey, quite how that one follows the trend eludes me, it was probably named after a session on the Mayhem, each of these beers had it's own distinctive flavour and characteristics.

During the four years that I had owned the pub we had served some two thousand different beers. Some of the breweries came up with imaginative and amusing names for their latest brews. Instead of the 'May' theme, Dent brewery apparently had a sheep fetishist for a brewer, since they were based in Cumbria, an area renowned for it's good looking sheep, he had named some of his beers after his first loves with titles such as Rambrau, Ramsbottom, T'owd Tup, Baa Baa of Seville and the incongruous KamiKaze. Summerskills brewery in Plymouth produced Whistlebelly Revenge, it's pump clip was resplendent with an enormous obese midriff somewhat akin to that of Aby's sibling. Cottage brewery in Somerset named their beers after trains or alternatively went down the whippet route with some of their brews being named after the brewery dog, this lead to names such as Jack the Whippet or Whacko Jacko. Cropton brewery in Pickering, North Yorkshire had a beer called Monksman's Slaughter, this was a very strong dark ale, it's name was the amalgamation of the brewer's and the drayman's surnames. Castle Rock brewery in Nottingham went down the wildlife trail, naming their brews after endangered species such as St John's Wort, Stickleback and Adder, they also produced a brew called Hemlock which for some obscure reason I could never get my wife to sample, strangely, she still ate the mushrooms. This brewery admirably donated money from each cask sold to support wildlife charities, thus the astute drinker could truthfully explain to his significant other, upon his late return home, that he had been assisting charities in their tireless task of fundraising.

Many beers were named in anticipation of sporting events such as cricket test matches or the football world cup, interestingly the brewers would often send two pump clips with the delivery. Usually one would proudly proclaim England's victory, the alternative and more frequently used back up announced that England had failed again. Similarly, Saints days produced an abundance of new beers, as did Christmas, with over 600 independent breweries in the UK, there was never a shortage of new beers to sample.

The licensee's trade, as I have hopefully illustrated, had some good points and some bad ones. The hours were long with few days off, moreover I had apparently become fair game for customer's derision and speculation, they took great delight in scrutinising my every move, they knew more about my life than I did. What they didn't know they made up. If I had done half the things which I allegedly had, I would have been a very happy if somewhat exhausted man, their intrusion into my private life was becoming a nuisance. I was bored and needed a new challenge in order to fulfil my aspirations.

When I first bought the business a close friend gave me a sound piece of advice. "Martyn" he said, so far so good, since after all that was my name, "Whatever you do, do not fuck the payroll". This statement needed no further explanation, diagrams or picture clues, it was as obvious as Mrs Blair's letterbox of a month, the most logical and comprehensible few words that one friend could give to another, to keep him on the straight road to loyalty and family bliss. To this day I do not know why I completely ignored his endeavours to enlighten me, but ignore it I did, and in true Langdale style, the brown, smelly, sticky stuff hit the large revolving object big style. Even Bill Clinton eventually surfaced from his little transgressions, smelling of roses, admittedly this made a welcome change from smelling of Monica's, however, it was highly unlikely that I would escape so lightly. No, unlike Bill, there was no point squirming and lying through my teeth in the best traditions of politicians, especially American ones. It would be futile saying 'Watch my lips, I did not have sex with that woman', I must have done it, I must be guilty as hell, they knew it, the whole town knew it, more importantly my wife knew it. Just for once the jungle telegraph was right, there was no point in denying it, no amount of lying would get me out of this shitty hole which I had dug for myself.

The lady in question was an adorable petite Scottish lassie from Troon, she had worked as an air hostess before the breakdown of her marriage had, seen her thrown in my general direction and deposited on my doorstep. She had worked for me for two years and for two years we had been an item, that's the way it was, two souls looking for something, not knowing exactly what or where it was, but at least we had found the map. At first we kept our relationship quiet, after all I was still married and married to the nicest lady in the world, who in 26 years had never once done anything to hurt me. I had ignored my friend's advice and jumped head first into the ubiquitous eternal triangle. I had tried in vain to balance the good points and bad points of each relationship, the carefree, happy and exciting feelings I was feeling for my new love against everything I had worked for during my 45 years on the planet with a woman who adored me and whose loyalty and integrity were never once called into question. This rapidly spinning world seemed to be accelerating faster with each new day. I was running as fast as I could and was getting nowhere, with the best intentions in the world I was a mess, most of my friends and family no longer wished to associate with me. Those who did had to face the wrath of their possessive and controlling partners, who apparently perceived that adultery, like leprosy and Ebola, was highly contagious. They stopped short of giving me a bell to ring on my travels, but only just. Furthermore, many of them made it all too clear that I was no longer a suitable drinking associate for their partners. It still intrigues me that whilst divorce seems to be a national sport at which we British do excel, it still feels like it's only ever happened to you, and that nobody knows the pain and heartache. Amazing really, since just about every man I know has at some time or other succumbed to the pleasures of another woman, some more than others, some made a habit of it, the lucky ones made a living out of it. Those who didn't were, it appeared, either dead, gay or just too fucking ugly

Note to self, and any other would be deviants, keep it tucked inside your trousers, it saves a lot of heartache. I learnt this the hard way, in the same way that I learned not to use a face cloth for its intended purpose, in someone else's bathroom, when I discovered that its owner, a fellow band member, did not use shit house paper. That the posh drinking fountain in my mates bathroom is not intended for such purposes, this I discovered when I learnt that, he too dispensed with such luxuries as toilet roll, and used it to wash his arse in, and finally, not to eat yellow snow, especially if the text is in your sisters handwriting.

Fortunately, my son had finally awoken to reality and his responsibilities, and was making a sterling effort in running the pub, gradually over the previous year, I had delegated more and more responsibility, and had taught him the finer points of cellar management, office skills, ordering, cleaning and necessary repairs all essential to a successful licensee's career. I knew the day would soon come when I would no longer be around, at least I had succeeded where the education system had failed and given junior a future in life, which would ensure his and his mother's financial security. I had been prudent, the business did not owe a penny to anybody, every brick, bottle and cask was paid for, my wife had a good job and the family home, so I took solace from the fact that she too would be well looked after, she most certainly did not deserve this shit and upheaval at a time in life when we should have been enjoying the rewards of our labours. However I knew I could not stay, I had not been living in the family home for some considerable time and I had lost my trust and respect for myself and my grip on reality. As a consequence of my actions my health was suffering, the only thing I had managed to nurture was a stomach ulcer, furthermore, I was becoming dangerously depressed. My depression was in no way alleviated when a close friend, who for the sake of anonymity will henceforth be referred to as 'Myers', with typical empathy, offered to lend me a rope to hang myself. Apparently, he did not recommend this course of action, since, some years earlier he had tried it himself, only to wake up in a hospital bed, in an embarrassed state, with nothing more to show for his troubles than a sore and slightly elongated neck, strangely Myers was also a publican. I should have known better that to take notice of him, since everything we did together ended in disaster, for example the day that he phoned to say he was going to take me to York races, in a mutual friends helicopter, private box, three course meal, free bar the works, sounded great. "I'll pick you up at 11" he said. "Fine" I replied, at approximately 11.15 the first helicopter to arrive at the helipad at Knavesmire, York was ours, and thus it was filmed by the television cameras from around the country, who were apparently tired of looking at the same piece of turf grow, whilst waiting for the days events to proceed. It promptly smashed into the ground at a great rate of knots from1500 feet, after smashing the underside of the aircraft it bounced back up into the air, narrowly missed flipping over and threw me through the door, not exactly the entrance I had envisaged. The ensuing CAA investigation declared the accident to be the result of a 'Vortex Ring', it did not however describe the effect which the accident had had upon my ring which has ever since refused to close properly and flutters uncontrollably at anything that even sounds like a helicopter, I duly determined that this was the one and only occasion in my life when my ring would be anywhere near the vicinity of a large chopper. As a result of the aircraft's untimely demise, we did however make the evening news bulletin. I am now a minor celebrity in my adopted city of York, as the nutter who crashed into the racecourse in £200,000 worth of Robinson R44 before blowing £300 on the horses. Since the only gambling I had ever attempted was debating whether or not I could outrun an irate husband with my jeans around my knees, whilst trying to repatriate my shirt, I knew nothing about the tipster's craft. I made the mistake of asking my trusted companion Myers, a veteran of many such jaunts for advice "Give me fifty quid" he said, my respect for the man was such that I did not question his instruction and duly handed over the money. "What do I do now" I asked. "Wait until the next race and give me another fifty quid" he replied. This monetary suicide continued all afternoon, not one winner, it was obvious that Myers knew less about horseracing than I did, typically people believed him, he was good with bullshit and had the ability to use big words. Furthermore, it was plain that this just was not going to be my day, I had apparently really pissed off the guy upstairs with my adulterous ways and, one way or another, he was going to make his disappointment in my errant ways very clear indeed.

On another occasion Myers and myself, together with a couple of good friends, nearly drowned off the east coast when our boat was swamped by a large wave and almost capsized, whilst out for a day's fishing. The fact that my friend, and owner of the boat had, for reasons best known to himself, decided to reverse the steering, did not help the potential disaster in the least, since the man was a professional lorry driver one would have expected that turning the wheel to the left would have resulted in something like a similar change in direction at the arse end of the vessel, apparently this fact had not even occurred to him and possibly goes some way to explaining why our motorways are full off such ignorant and incapable drivers, whose major contributions to society seem to be to cause avoidable traffic jams with a resultant rise in mortality rates from the ensuing carnage which they are so adept at causing. Fortunately the only casualties on this occasion were our collective pride and Myers' mobile phone. The man is just an accident waiting to happen. He had once flown his single engined plane into the paddock behind his house, not literally as was the case with the helicopter in York, but for once he landed it safely, as per the instruction manual. Unfortunately, at the time, he had not contemplated how he would extricate his pride and joy and repatriate it to its usual residence on the local air strip, in short he had failed to notice that the paddock was not of sufficient length to allow him to take off again. Despite several failed attempts at take off from his impromptu airstrip, he, in his own words, 'bottled it' due, in no small part, to the presence of overhead cables and a not insubstantial wooden fence. Fortunately, he was well connected with various people who mattered in such circumstances and presently the RAF came to his rescue with a Chinook helicopter, at considerable expense to the taxpayer, they promptly rigged a series of slings under the stranded aircraft and duly returned it, much to his embarrassment and relief. If it had tits or engines it was sure to land Myers in deep trouble. On reflection, it was a pity that he had sadly failed in his half hearted attempt at suicide and neck stretching, since it would undoubtedly have saved a lot of time, money and trouble, for the poor unfortunates who had the misfortune to cross his path. His command of middle English was impeccable, since he had a degree in the subject, but his comprehension of all things involving an internal combustion engine was at best naïve and at worst bloody dangerous, quite why I ever chose the man as a shooting partner defies even the most basic logic, although, as he pointed out, the local gun club, of which he was president, had only ever shot one person, and since he was a solicitor, that hardly mattered.

It was a fine summer's day in Gainsborough, I was outside the pub cleaning my bike, a gleaming BMW GS1100 as ridden by Ewan McGregor on his round the world escapades. I observed not one, but two patrol cars as they rolled into the car park and duly parked up. The local bookies had closed all bets on what would happen next. The two ambassadors of the British legal system approached me, if only they had arrived in such numbers and been so confident two weeks previously, I could have avoided the confrontation with the local peg dealing fraternity. The officer who eventually arrived on that day then cautioned me for causing a breach of the peace and distressing a police officer. If ever I needed a demonstration of the failings of the system, this was it. Two weeks prior I had been assaulted by three inebriated low life pieces of giro cashing, tarmac laying scum, the police, as usual, allowed the situation to sort itself out before venturing near, a little like the Americans in 1941, not wanting to get involved or deal with the ensuing paper work, and now I was the easy target who was going to pay the price, just to keep plods crime solving figures up to a point where he could justify his shambolic contribution to law and order. It was apparent that if I, together with a few carefully selected regulars, had dealt with the situation ourselves, I would by now be sitting in the same interview room facing a charge of grievous bodily harm, it was a win, win situation for the crown, I didn't stand a chance. The outcome of the situation was similarly predictable, I received an £80 ASBO. In forty five years on the planet, I had never deliberately broken the laws of the land and until now had considered myself to be an upright, law abiding citizen who would erupt in a fit of rage upon observing some cretin drop a piece of litter, things were going to change, what was the point of being straight in this country if this was the result. The police were happy, they had a result, the perpetrators of the incident were no doubt oblivious and blissfully happy knowing that the state would not want to infringe their human rights as an ethnic minority, despite the fact that in Gainsborough they were the majority.

I read somewhere that the male Gypsy moth can smell the female Gypsy moth from a distance of up to a mile, this sentence also works if you remove the word moth, as you may be aware I am not an ardent admirer of the genre. My only act of retaliation to the officer involved, who will remain nameless, but will henceforth be known as 'PC Custard' i.e. an amalgamation of a C you next Tuesday and a bastard, was to inform him that I had mistakenly believed that the two of us were supposed to be on the same side when it came to keeping law and order in town, and that my sincere wish was that on his return home that evening he should discover the low lifes in question removing anything of value from his property before buggering his pet dog and anally violating his wife and offspring. If the poor mite was distressed by my actions and words, God knows what effect such a discovery would have on him, I cannot help thinking that if he was so sensitive maybe he had chosen the wrong career path and would have been more suited to a vocation in the library service, perhaps he was bullied a lot at nursery or had an over protective mother. I suggested that his colleagues would probably appear on the scene a damned sight more rapidly for him, than he had done for me. Furthermore, I told him he could stick the invitation to his parents wedding where the sun didn't shine. I figured that I was off his Christmas card list for good and strongly suspected that any further recourse to the law would be met with similar lethargy.

This was the final straw which broke the back of my addled brain, coupled with the comedy of errors which my private life had become and my growing disdain for the shambles that was once the greatest nation on the planet. I decide it was time to join the thousands of like minded exiles of this green and unpleasant land and play ostrich for a while, that is, bury my head in some distant sand, preferably as far away from Gainsborough as was possible, since the bus to Mars was apparently full I prescribed myself a brief respite period across the channel.

FRANCE

As I opened the lilac painted slatted shutters of the villa my skin was bathed by the warmth of the morning sun, the thermometer read 24'C and the sky was washed with a deep azure blue which highlighted the myriad of pastel colours of the surrounding windows and doors of the neighbouring properties, each topped with a collage of russet and ochre pan tiles perched on sun bleached white walls. The Aroma of pine woods and newly mown grass hung in the warm breeze as the frogs sang a serenade from the overhanging wisteria branches.

Thanks to Mr Bush and co, and their unending mission to warm the world for us lesser mortals in temperate climates, I suppose that I could have been in England in April, in truth I was in the south of France at the end of November, about thirty minutes drive from St Tropez, sipping the days first freshly ground coffee and drinking in the beautiful vista before me.

This was my first time in France, although I knew that I had arrived for two reasons. Firstly, the pilot of the Boeing 737 aircraft which delivered me, had a flight deck replete with computers and navigational aids at his disposal and thus would have had to be pretty stupid to land in the wrong country, I hypothesized that even Stevie Wonder on a bad day could have delivered me to my destination using modern satellite navigation systems; assuming of course that the local hoodies hadn't nicked his Tom-Tom off the dashboard. Secondly, the scene that greeted me as the arrival lounge doors opened, could only happen in France.

I pondered what it was about doorways that made women want to stand and talk, usually whilst being in charge of a supermarket trolley, and wondered what was wrong with the acres of space a few nanoseconds away, as I started to walk towards the exit doors. Started, that is, because within a couple of steps through the mobile chicane, a fully grown canine spontaneously erupted from my left leg, it had a fully grown tongue and a fully grown pair of biceps and it had determined that now would be a convenient time to greet me in the time honoured 'doggy fashion', or not as the case may be. "Pardonné moi" shouted the lady of a certain age, who was stood all of 20 metres away, initially bewildered, I realised that the dog which at one end was firmly attached to my leg was attached at the other by an unfeasibly long nylon leash, quite why I did not understand, the dog had enough freedom to nip to the beach, watch a video, shag a few legs and return without it's owner ever realising. Just the sort of thing for a busy arrivals lounge I mused, as I resisted the temptation to kick its balls into the middle of next week.

I was later to learn that the dogs in France are not proper dogs, rather they are Peter Pan dogs which never grow larger than an anorexic Yorkshire terrier with a sixty a day habit and a hormone imbalance. Apparently, it is the law in

France that there are two ways of walking a dog, the first, as mentioned, is by means of an unfeasibly long lead, the second and seemingly the most preferred method is to carry the said dog in an under the arm manner, I never did discover why, after all evolution had blessed most dogs with a leg at each corner. For a while I assumed the dogs were being used as armpit merkins to keep the more debonair ladies warm, but later I noticed that most of them had sufficient hair of their own in that particular area and figured that the dogs, like their owners, were just fucking lazy! It also bothered me, somewhat, that the dogs were all better dressed than I was.

Still mentally scarred from my canine violation, I fought my way through the walking wounded of the local Derby and Joan branch, who had survived the passage and were now intent on greeting long lost relatives from previous missions by pecking them on each cheek like rabid woodpeckers head banging to a 'Hawkwind' album, and found my way to the bar.

The bartender was smoking a cigarette, I ordered a 'croquet monsieur' and a cool beer, the glass had 25ml stamped on the side, I received about 12.5 ml, the cigarette never left Pierre's mouth. If I was Pierre and had been in England, I mused cynically, I would by now have been surrounded by a pen toting army of customs and excise officials, environment health officers and the bureaucratic thought police, and would be inundated by a plethora of closure orders and fines, but this was France and as I was to repeatedly discover, the only laws that the French adhered to were either ones they liked or ones which began with the words 'would you like another 10 billion Euros Mr minister in order that you may give your hard working peasant farmers more subsidies and extend their unfeasibly long lunch breaks', it was overtly obvious that Pierre did not give a flying fuck for European laws and probably thought that the common market was where his mother did her shopping on a Saturday morning!

It was around this time that I noticed the adolescents parading around the arrivals lounge, dressed as police officers and admiring the days acne growth in their window reflections, they had uniforms just like the real article and, to top off the illusion, they had a toy gun in a holster. Perhaps they desired to be real policemen when they grew up, I thought, then slowly the centime dropped, they were the real thing, fully loaded with 9mm pistols. Somewhere along the way, I mused, I must have slipped into a 'time and space continuum' and lost touch with reality, I remember thinking, I have a twenty year old son, which made him about twice as old as spotty plod, and I would not trust him with anything more dangerous than a rubber knife and a set of plastic toy handcuffs, never mind a lethal weapon, it's just plain dangerous and asking for trouble, in my opinion. The things the youth of today have to do to supplement their pocket money and keep themselves in hard drugs and alcohol. In England, these chaps would not have been served with a pack of fags at the local store, but again, this was France, I pictured the scene at the local Bar Tabac "how many disc bleu's was it again Pierre, two hundred, merci?"

The first thing I noticed about the cars in France was that without exception each was dented, scratched or had a piece missing, apparently it is the law, probably. One night, whilst walking to my favourite restaurant in St Raphael, I purposefully checked every parked car for damage, I estimated that approximately 90% had battle scars, the remainder were just right offs. The reason for this soon became apparent, when I witnessed Jean DeBastard attempt to park his Rover 400 into a space the size of Victoria Beckham's cleavage, a smart car with an eating disorder would not have fitted into the space, even if it was lowered in by crane, not that that deterred Jean in the slightest, he just banged from side to side like a deranged tennis ball on an Absinthe and acid trip, until he reached the point where even he had to admit that he would not be able to fit, what was by now a significantly shorter vehicle, into the available space, C'est la vie, n'est pas.

I soon learned that French drivers consider extras, such as mirrors, indicators, doors etc to be superfluous and an inconvenience, after all they never used them, and thus whenever possible they tried to remove them by whatever means available, be it a wall, another car or a person, stationary or moving, they just didn't give a toss.

On the drive from St Tropez to the villa there is a beautiful stretch of road that winds up the hills from the village through steeply rising pine forests to the top of the pass before descending to the golden sands of the cote d'Azure. The road snakes sharply downwards with no kerbs or barriers to prevent the inattentive driver from proving Newton's laws in a most graphic manner before crashing to certain annihilation in the valley below. In order to make the drive a little more interesting the French road builders decided to put a 3ft deep gulley approximately 6 inches from the edge. I was aware of Alain Prost's grandfather in his battered white Citroen C15 van, minus mirrors, the odd wing and indicators as he came thundering down the mountain behind me, lights flashing and horn blaring, at the time there were two other cars diligently following at a polite distance, but that didn't stop Mr Prost senior from over taking both of them on the winding hairpin bends, before he used the same inane manoeuvre on myself, on yet another blind bend. I wondered at his apparent longevity and pondered what would have happened in 1940 if his ancestors had been as equally aggressive. Then it was the turn of the car in front, the sharp left hander turned into a sharp right, the little van pulled out on the blind bend, the tyres, all 3 inches of them, tried to part company with the rims as he raced by, totally oblivious of any danger to himself or anybody else, by the time I had turned the corner he had gone. I never did discover if he had disappeared down the abyss or if he had slotted a twin turbo Ferrari engine under the bonnet and was on his way to Le Mans for a quick road test, followed by a large Ricard and the obligatory fag.

This driving technique I could have understood from a high flying city trader who was about to make millions from a deal in some foreign country and was rushing down the M1 on a busy Friday night to catch a connection at Heathrow, but this was rural France, where the locals took three hours for lunch before closing up shop and going home for tea, without a doubt they are one of the few nations on planet Earth who make the Spanish appear industrious.

Apparently, the only reason to rush anywhere in France is to play Boules, it is compulsory to play every day, probably. The rules state that a player must be at least 65 years old and he must have carried out a 10 year apprenticeship in smoking. The object of the game is to throw an unfeasibly heavy ball at an unfeasibly small ball, preferably knocking the opponents balls into the next parish, the winner gets a Disc Bleu and a kiss on both cheeks, look out for it on Sky Sports it's riveting end to end action, all that it is missing are the cheerleaders, excitement and a sprinkling of gratuitous violence.

Saturday morning in St Tropez was market day, I dutifully climbed inside my hire car, a Peugeot 309 to make the pilgrimage. I had become quite attached to this particular piece of French engineering on account of the fact that it switched on it's own lights when it became dark, assuming of course that they were still attached to the vehicle, it wiped the screen automatically if it rained and drank about as much as a strict Methodist trying to climb a few more steps to the big man, it also had a pretty fluorescent display which told me what the temperature was, what day it was, how much fuel I hadn't used etc, I fully expected that if I left the bathroom door open in the morning it would quietly saunter in and wipe my arse. Clever bastards these French, unfortunately I guessed it would be a certain bet that it would either break, or fall apart, the day after the guarantee expired.

I soon learned why French cars do so many things automatically for the driver, it is because in France you need 110% concentration to get to your destination in one piece. For a start the French drive on the wrong side of the road, a fact which I soon discovered they were blissfully unaware of, secondly they have a strange habit of placing road signs after junctions, this means that you are aware that you have gone the wrong way but cannot rectify the situation until you return to see the sign that should have been pointing in the opposite direction before the junction, then the whole game starts again, simple!. Perhaps this anomaly was a throw back to the war and served to confuse uncle Adolf and crew, when he was on his jollies to Paris circa 1940, or perhaps the French just like to take the piss out of the tourists, lets face facts, they never really forgave us for Agincourt, cheese eating surrender monkeys, every last one.

The markets in France were fantastic, admittedly I preferred the ones in India where there was more blood, guts and shit than Europe, with a bit of slaughter thrown in for effect and to keep the casual observer interested. In France the stalls were a kaleidoscope of colour with fruit and vegetables of every conceivable variety and colour, all freshly picked that morning by local growers, and were thus as fresh as Sister Virginia's cotton gussets. The smell of meat cooking on the spits filled the warm air, the array of cooked meats and the infinite variety of superb cheeses were a joy of which I never tired, the aromas of new baked bread and roasting chestnuts, spicy sausages and Parma hams floated through the bustling crowds, it was a bluebottles paradise, every stall a one stop free for all for Mr and Mrs fly and family, as with everything else in France, nobody seemed to mind the flies, even the horse which was being ridden past the trailer proudly advertising 'Viende de Cheval' didn't seem too bothered about his ultimate destiny, perhaps he just thought 'I'm sure that's uncle Ned on that slab, never did like him anyway, always was horsing about'.

The market square in St Tropez was surrounded by café bars and restaurants, I chose one and sat down with the locals to participate in the most popular leisure activity in France, people watching. The French excelled at this pastime, and so they should for they practised for at least

3 hours a day, four if they were not too busy. In November, most of the locals had left town, after all it was only twenty odd degrees and thus far too cold for them, the remainder, who soldiered on and bravely battled the elements, paraded around town in thick woollens, coats, scarves, FMB's and mini skirts, the women that is, with the obligatory dog or two under each arm. I simply sat by the pavement in shirt sleeves and sweated it out whilst letching at the profusion of attractive ladies and the bustling scene which unfolded before me. In France even the ladies of a certain age looked good, they exuded an air of elegance and decorum, except obviously when the toy poodle had puked down their best fur coat. My attention was drawn to a lady who was wearing an overly tight pair of denim jeans and sat immediately in front of me, that's nice I dribbled to myself, whilst considering the notion that a few extra sutures in her 'camel's hoof' would not have gone a miss. At this point she leaned forwards to reveal the hairiest bum crack and lower back that I had ever encountered in the female form, despite the fact that I have worked on several building sites and am good friends with a couple of bricklayers, what a way to shatter the illusion, I thought, still nice arse. The French really were a hairy race. During my entire stay in France I only ever bumped into, metaphorically speaking, one obese woman, I later discovered that she was from Wakefield so she didn't really count, she was deftly dodging the mopeds which madly zipped up and down

the street like deranged lemmings, and enquiring of the locals, 'Ou est le chip shop'. Obviously, she sported the requisite number of cheap tattoos and had gone to the trouble of embellishing her matted peroxide locks with a bright pink streak, as is apparently de rigour with the informed modern fat bird who wishes to draw attention to her aversion for salads and her problematic body odour and is convinced that five a day refers to the number of family packs of crisps to be eaten before the conclusion of daytime TV.

I marvelled at the agility of the bars' dog as it deftly stood on three legs, licked itself deftly around it's more than ample set of bollocks, and scratched it's flea bitten arse with the remaining leg, before picking up a rancid sausage from the gutter and proudly trotting off towards it's master's car, where it promptly jumped up, checked inside the vehicle and, realising that he wasn't there, lay down to wait for him and enjoy it's newly found meal.

The French produce some fantastic wines for approximately two pence per hectolitre, furthermore, coffee is half the price it is in the UK, which begs the question, why do the French cafes and bars insist on serving both drinks in ridiculously small vessels. The coffee is served in Alice in Wonderland's cast off thimbles, which are so small that it is impossible to get a finger in the handle, (I am thinking Sister Virginia again, but in the interests of decency and a possible libel case, the less said the better, the last thing I need now is a law suit from the Catholic church) and similarly the wine is served in ridiculously small measures. Why? Most of the cost of production is paid for by the British tax payer via grants and subsidies in any event, the very least that the big nosed bastards could do is to serve a decent sized measure.

The first thing that the virgin visitor observes on entering a shop in France is that it is closed, they are nocturnal beasties which open when normal shops close, and still the owners take three hours for lunch. If you are lucky enough to find one open, the first thing that the customer is likely to notice is that the proprietor always says 'Hello' in a polite heartfelt way, similar to the Americans 'Have a nice day', except the French mean it, where as the Americans really mean 'I want to napalm your kids and bum your dog now give me some money motherfucker'.

The French know a thing or two about food, even the humblest bar or café serves great food at a fraction of the price of the UK, at Nimes airport it is possible to obtain a three course meal with a carafe of wine for less than £10, try doing that at Heathrow, if you are lucky you may just be able to afford a 'Big Mac, lovely. In fact the locals use the airport just for the restaurant, and seem a little bemused that the place is overrun with planes and passengers. On the occasion that I was there, the restaurant was full of local business people taking three hours for lunch and dodging oversexed dogs.

You have to hand it to a nation who can make cows' innards, horses' dicks, frog's legs and slugs taste good. Sometimes they don't even bother with the cooking part of cooking and just throw the food on to the plate. In my favourite restaurant in Roquebroune, 'The Gespachio', they serve a fantastic Carpaccio of beef or salmon, served on a fresh bed of rocket with lemon and still warm bread, baked that afternoon. I wondered what the residents of Blighty, brought up on a diet of Big Macs, kebabs and micro waved ready meals would think of this veritable gourmets treasure chest of culinary delights, possibly something like, I'm not putting that in my mouth. (Ssr Virginia?) One evening, in the same restaurant, my friend ordered steak tartar, 'No Cook' said the waitress in broken English, obviously thinking 'stupid English Bastard' the fact that my friend is a Polish chef who speaks fluent French appeared irrelevant. At which point, I mused, did the chef who invented this particular dish think that it would be a spiffing idea to serve a pound of raw minced beef with a raw egg on top. Perhaps it was a local 'who can contract the most salmonella and botulism contest' which initiated his idea, or perhaps he was just late for a champion boules match. Maybe he was rushing to his uncles funeral, the man having sadly died whilst attempting to off road his Citroen van down a hillside after missing the apex off a blind bend on the road to St Maxime, or perhaps he was just late for his unfeasibly long lunch break and thought 'If sir wants a beef burger, then sir can bloody well cook it himself', before slamming the plate on to the table with the words 'I'm off'. Sir, probably in a similar rush to take his wife's fur coat to the cleaners to have the contents of Fifi's stomach removed, probably thought 'What the hell, I'm hungry, here goes, waitress may I have a Spanish egg please I prefer the extra salmonella'. The idea caught on and thus we have steak tartar on the menu, not that any- one with half a brain would want to eat the shit. Personally I would rather suck off the local tramp through a sweaty piss stained sock than sink to such depths of depravity.

Roquebrune is a quaint archetypal French village set at the foot of a massive rock outcrop, hence its name. It's narrow cobbled streets meander up the hillside through ancient gate houses and beautiful Provencal four and five story houses, to the small market square with it's fountains and imposing church, definitely picture postcard material. In truth, that is where I learned what the village looked like, since on the numerous occasions when I paraded its ancient streets, I never once dared to look upwards at the architecture which had stood there for hundreds of years. This was partly due to the French law that each person must own at least one dog, which must at all times leave its recycled pedigree chum on the streets, and partly because although the French have mastered great technical achievements such as; half tunnelling under the channel, half building concord or discovering how to create cars that know when it is dark or wet, they have never managed the relatively simple task of producing shit shovels or plastic dog poo bags, or maybe the usual rule applies, they just don't give a damn about anyone else. If the streets of London are paved with gold, the streets of Roquebrune are paved with shit, mountains of the stuff, this results in the local residents participating in the little known sport of Roquebrune hopscotch, or dodging the shit as David Blunket would say, (I wonder who picks his guide dog's shit up, surely he cannot be that good? I wonder if blind people can buy Braille dog shit bags?) beware the hopscotch player who looks up for a brief moment to view the oppositions progress or look at the woman in front with the beard and hairy bum crack. I later discovered that this game was played in many towns and villages, but not in St Tropez where killjoy council operatives pressure wash the streets, with perfumed detergent, which makes the whole area smell like a cheap tarts boudoir, apparently. On one occasion, I was walking through the back streets of St Maxime, I was following a couple who were walking hand in hand perusing the closed shop windows, when suddenly they stopped and pointed animatedly at the pavement, the man then proceeded to imitate the mating call of a sex starved donkey which had just spent 6 months in solitary confinement at the local donkey sanctuary with Mrs 'I love it up me donkeyess' in 'season' in the adjoining cell. Eeyaw, eeyaw he bellowed and continued to bellow, by which time I was prostrate on the pavement, being careful, as always, to avoid Trixie's little presents, whilst thinking, even for a Frenchman this behaviour cannot be normal. The man continued his donkey impressions all the way down the street, slowly I understood his actions, he was alerting the rest of his entourage to the dangers underfoot, every time he spied a turd he went into rampant donkey imitation mode. I remember thinking if he does that every time he sees a pile of shit around here, he's going to be a little hoarse in the morning.

It was shortly after this bizarre visual and audible display that I discovered Willy Wonkers canine division, it intrigued my sick imagination to such an extent that I felt duty bound to investigate further. I do not know what the French feed their canine friends, but a walk around the perimeter of St Mixime's municipal car park is most enlightening to the average deviant and shit connoisseur, it is festooned with snickers bars, with real nuts, walnut whips in the most surreal and difficult to reach places, Maltesers and the occasional double Twix, in short dog shit of every shape, colour and consistency, although I cannot comment on the taste since I had a cold at the time. For sure, Willy would have been proud of his oompalumpa's selection of lumps. On the downside, I didn't observe a single piece of white shitolate, which as any faecal connoisseur knows is the holy grail of shit, sadly now almost extinct, perhaps it went the same way as dark chocolate Mars bars, perhaps, there just wasn't the demand.

Conversely, a walk around the streets of Gainsborough, reveals pavements smeared with the remnants of faecal violations where their owners have made a half hearted attempt at cleaning up the semi solid products of Fido's digestive tract. Thus unequivocally proving the well known computer acronym 'GIGO, i.e., garbage in, garbage out, in other words if Fido is fed crap he will inevitably shit crap out of the other end, personally I have never fed my dog anything which I would not eat myself, although I do have the luxury of not living on benefits and do not to the best of my knowledge have a serious Heroin addiction, I also have the benefit of being able to easily pick up solid stools. In truth, most of the dog owners merely left the contents of pooch's stomach where they fell, along with their used syringes, Special Brew cans and used Macdonald's wrappers.

The morning sun was beaming as I walked the hill to the pharmacy, the streets, as always were quiet. Outside a small cottage sat an elderly man brandishing on old side by side 12 bore shotgun, barrels resting across his knees, he eyed me closely. To be on the safe side I motioned towards him 'Bonjour monsieur,' I said in my best broad Yorkshire/French accent, and forlornly hoped that he wouldn't notice that I was English. I had formed the opinion that the French did not particularly like Johnny Angleterre, strange I thought, since if it wasn't for my ancestors they would all be speaking German, wearing Lederhosen and driving BMWs or Porsches. Perhaps that is why they don't like the English, at least Hitler would have cleaned up the dog shit and gassed the culprits I thought, presumably, their choice of vehicles would also have been more robust and a damned sight more reliable if the allies hadn't triumphed, circa 1945.

I entered the pharmacy and attempted to purchase my requirements. 'Bonjour monsieur' I said to the young man behind the counter 'avez vous du Canesten', Pierre looked at me with a totally blank expression 'Quest que ce' he replied, the two ladies behind the counter had started to take an interest in my embarrassment and ineptitude with the indigenous language, I realised that this was going to be more difficult than I had anticipated. 'Monsieur, avez vous du crème pour mon knob' I didn't know the French for prick; apart from Sarkozy which I guessed would only complicate the problem, furthermore I didn't know whether it should be a male or female gender i.e. mon or ma, and frankly I didn't care, I just wanted to get some relief for my burning member ,and vacate the chemist as quickly as possible, I hadn't felt like this since I was fifteen and went into the Late shopper to buy condoms, only to return with a bottle of Lucozade and some phlegm cream. 'Monsieur, Mon knob c'est un feu' I tried again, pointing to my reddened appendage, who until very recently had been my best mate.

'Ah, oui' replied the pharmacist, the two ladies behind the counter were by now pissing themselves, in French of course. Pierre produced a tube of cream, just as well, since by this time my face was the same colour as my best mates balaclava, i.e. bright crimson. I now feel fully qualified to give the casual traveller to France a helpful little tip, If you need to visit a chemist in France and suffer from dubious near vision, take a pair of reading glasses with you. I returned to the villa, dodging the usual doggy doos and donned said glasses. It was at this moment that I realised Pierre had successfully sold me a tube of athletes foot cream, the bastard. Perhaps his grandfather was at Crecy, no wonder the women behind the counter were so amused. Not to worry I thought, technically my best mate is not a foot, but what's half an inch between friends, surprisingly, the cream did the job and comfort was restored, no more whistling song birds in my pants. Incidentally, Pierre scored double Brownie points in the morning when I attempted to clean my teeth with the stuff, at least I won't get fungal infections in my gums. On leaving the chemist I noticed a Durex machine on the outside wall of the chemist, I wondered how long it would have stayed there had it been in England. I tried to envisage who would have the balls to use such a machine in full public view. Try as I may, I just couldn't picture Jean Claud aged sixteen rolling up with his mates on their mopeds shouting the words, 'just a minute lads I need to get some condoms for Claudette before my mum sees me', it just wouldn't happen, there isn't even the Lucozade and phlegm medicine option, to use as an excuse.

So there it is, my brief synopsis of rural life in France, great food, great wines, nice weather, classy hairy women, cars that think for themselves, crap dogs, dogs craps and weird sports. A land where nobody gives a shit and it's OK to park wherever you want, outwardly I loath the French, secretly I admire and envy them their laid back lifestyle, as I left St Tropez, I bumped into Alain Prost. 'Bonjour Al' I said, 'nice car, did you get the dents yourself, incidentally, watch that dog shit on your tyres'. Apparently he had been for a spin around Monte Carlo, the wrong way round. 'How's the knob' he enquired – big nosed bastard!

SCHOOL

One of the unexpected bonuses of being in France, was that for the first time in my life I was able to reflect upon my life thus far, and attempt to understand why I was in the desperate situation in which I now found myself, and try to ascertain at which point I had pressed the large red self destruct button. Langdale the movie would, most certainly, be found in the disaster section of the local video store. I tried to visualise which decisions had precipitated the feelings of guilt, anger and frustration that I now felt and understand what events had initiated my successes and failures. In my mind I tried to piece together the jigsaw which had made me the person I was, as was always the case with jigsaws there were a few crucial pieces missing.

My memories of Braithwell County Primary School, located between Rotherham and Doncaster, were to say the least vague, for some inexplicable reason although the rest of my body seemed to be functioning in an acceptable manner, my memory did not properly kick start itself until around my early teens, strangely enough this was also the time when I first began to notice the members of the opposite sex and the relative differences there in. The school was tiny, it had four classrooms and approximately 100 pupils, half way through my stay I recall that we were given the luxury of indoor toilets, previously we had had to make the journey across the playground to the small toilet block situated outside in the yard, unfortunately this new era of sanitary luxury and innovation was not coupled with the benefit of soft toilet tissue, we were still expected to make do with the standard issue Izal shiny paper, which was to bum wiping what Stephen Hawkins was to the international athletics scene, and which displayed a readiness to slide up the unwary wipers back with all the finesse of Bambi on ice, furthermore it was all too easily pierced by an errant digit more used to it's softer cousin. It was also responsible for indelibly stamping the inimitable sentence, 'now wash your hands' on my embryonic memory.

I have a less than lucid memory of my first tentative steps in my musical career. when I was given the task of being first trianglist (is there such a word?) in the weekly 'Music and Movement' sessions. This imaginatively titled series, produced for television, entailed each pupil in the class, both male and female, removing most of their clothes and gyrating about on the classroom floor in front of the monochrome TV set, whilst sidestepping potatoes, carrots, peas and other such debris that were left from the days lunch, with hindsight I am now convinced that the whole shebang was an early attempt at organized paedophilia with just a hint of sadism thrown in for good measure, although I cannot remember if Mr Savile was the DJ. The only pupil spared the humiliation was the poor unfortunate who nature determined should wear a pair of leg callipers, to be fair this seemed like a reasonable excuse, I don't think he wore them for effect. The session was a cross between PT and Ti Chi, with a smattering of obscure music thrown in for dramatic effect, Imagine getting five year old pupils to participate in such debauched orgies of the flesh today, any teacher naïve enough to try would soon be learning the lines to 'Do you wanna touch me' tutored by none other than the great Mr Glitter himself in his cosy little cell, whilst being extended the hospitality of one of Her Majesty's finest institutions. Since those early days of deviancy, I have never again been able to recreate such hedonistic rituals, at least not on such an expansive scale, involving such large numbers of participants, without recourse to copious amounts of alcohol and/or mind expanding drugs. If I had progressed to become the leader of a strange religious sect which worshipped oversized lingerie, any psychologist worth their salt, would have traced my embryonic debauchery to these sessions. Fortunately, as befitted the school milk monitor, I did not allow myself to be corrupted by such depraved filth and took my new found responsibility seriously, even at this early stage in my development my peers were obviously aware that I was a leader of men and was thus more than capable of dishing out the one third of a pint milk bottles which were deposited every morning on the front step of the school. Obviously, this was pre-Thatcherite times before she preformed her Marie Antoinette on steroids impression and uttered the immortal words 'let the peasants die of rickets or some other vitamin deficient disease' allegedly. In my mind she was not so much 'Thatcher, Thatcher the milk snatcher' as 'Thatcher the tight fisted Tory Twat' who wrecked the lives of the working class communities in which I was raised, although to be fair she taught the Argies a thing or two about modern warfare and how to retain the sovereignty of a few sheep infested islands miles from anywhere, furthermore she would undoubtedly have shown the bunch of unelected parasites in Brussels who was queen bitch, and no doubt have twatted Angela Merkel about the laughing gear with her hand bag. How ironic, I mused, that whilst our troops were being shot at, miles from home, in an attempt to secure the mineral wealth of the Falklands, her cabinet was doing it's utmost to close every mine, steelworks and industrial plant in it's own country.

Another inexplicable memory which I have retained from my formative school days, was the smell of latex rubber glue, for what reason still eludes me. If only I had nurtured this innate tendency, I could doubtless have become a leading exponent of the latex fetishist's art, unfortunately I apparently lost my way and never attained my true potential in this particular field of deviancy, now the smell only serves to remind me of the many painful hours I spent in the dentist's chair with an anaesthetic mask strapped to my face after eating too many sherbet dips and penny chews.

I recall that the beginning and end of break time was signalled by the headmaster ringing a small brass hand bell from the school steps. I remember the aroma of coffee that drifted from the staffroom doorway, this was the place where the school nurse would periodically check the pupils heads for lice, on her visits and would administer various inoculations, if only there had been an anti-adultery vaccine available, my life would have been so much easier, but a damned sight more boring. I recall also the smell of pipe tobacco and watching the headmaster contemplatively puffing away, perhaps this is where I contracted the pipe smoking habit for it is one of life's pleasures which I still enjoy, despite the best efforts of his royal Tonyness and crew, although I do not recall taking a pipe to class at the tender age of six. In these sanitised, litigant times the average school pupil would probably have more chance of seeing a flock of Dodos roosting on the classroom window ledge, than see the head teacher stoke up before them. Thank goodness that our omnipotent peers have now covered the brightly coloured tobacco products on retailer's shelves in an attempt to dissuade any would be smoker from indulging in the dark art. What insight and knowledge our elected guardians exhibit on occasions, whilst their efforts may thwart the local magpie population's smoking, they are doubtful to make one iota of difference to a seasoned smoker with a forty a day habit, for sure the reason why people indulge, has sweet

F.A. to do with pretty coloured packaging and more to do with nicotine requirements. Wake up you bunch of interfering arseholes, believe me, if the extortionate amount of revenue which the treasury receives in the form of taxation, does little to deter them, no amount of cancerous gum photographs, gangrenous legs and health warnings will succeed, especially when they see the country's increasing number of obese citizens not been taxed in a similar manner when they consume excessive amounts of cholesterol laden fast food, fizzy drinks and snacks, whilst piling on the stones. I would venture to suggest that these members of society will likewise cost the nation billions in healthcare and benefit payments, apart from looking a fucking mess when they waddle down the street with muffin tops hanging over their jogging bottoms and the rear end of an under exercised, fishnet adorned milking cow dangling from the bottom of their mini skirt, in Gainsborough the women are not much better.

My headmaster was certainly a character, his name was Mr Brooks, apart from his obvious prowess at pipe smoking he was also an accomplished concertina player and raconteur, One would doubtless imagine that with these sought after abilities he would have been an absolute hoot at parties, strangely and inexplicably, he had acquired an alternative alphabet which to the best of my recollections went something like; A for horses, B for mutton, C for fish, F you any eggs, L for leather, P before bedtime, Q for chocolates, T for two, U for me, X for breakfast etc, this obviously made such an impression that, even today I can still recall some of his words after a gap of some forty years, although, frankly what fucking good this knowledge has done me is still open to debate. Let's be honest, it is hardly likely to be part of a modern curriculum, as indeed is anything involving the alphabet or numbers if the lefty do goody box tickers get their way.

The only recollection I have from my six years at primary school, was being moved by the vicar, to the front seats of the church, during the harvest festival as a result of misbehaving, this was obviously an omen for my future misdemeanours and resulted in my great distrust of balding grown men who wore black dresses and white collars in public. My family had never been big on religion and the whole gig seemed a little contrived to my young reasoning, with hindsight this was probably the time when the almighty took a dislike to me for acting about at his gaff, and where the seeds of atheism were firmly implanted in my head. I was also given an early grounding in the theory of hypocrisy when the vicars' wife ran off with another man from the village, if the family of a man of the cloth was not immune to temptations of the flesh, how was a mere mortal like myself supposed to cope? It was readily apparent that my life would be an uphill struggle, and that shit would inevitably happen.

Maltby Grammar School was the complete antithesis of my earlier place of education, it was situated in a mining town in the Peoples republic of South Yorkshire and, like a Philippino back street cafe, had a reputation for being a dog eat dog environment, especially since it had ceased to be a Grammar school the year previous to my induction, and now had to accept the 'poor people', with their inherent diseases, into its hallowed halls. I was plunged violently from a tiny rural haven into the third largest school in the country, with some two thousand pupils, like a sacrificial lamb to the slaughter, not to put too fine a point on it, I was shitting myself. Fortunately, my memory had decided that it would grasp hold of the job in hand and had deemed that it would take notice of the world for future reference. Pain, I find has a habit of being an efficient catalyst in such cases.

The pain which I was feeling at the time was, I recall, as a direct result of being inverted through 180 degrees and placed head first into a large rubbish bin, my first cursory glances at Maltby Grammar school were not so much through rose tinted spectacles, but more through the sharp and unforgiving wire mesh of the receptacles base. I was plunged head first into an Antipodean, upside-down world where classrooms grew downwards from the sky and my fellow pupils walked around on the ceiling. Later in the day, after extricating myself from the bin, I discovered that I had fared reasonably well in the ritual initiation ceremony proceedings, which were eagerly administered by the older pupils. Several of my colleagues, I use the term rather than friends since I knew precisely six people in this vast educational metropolis, had suffered the indignation of either being thrown, fully clothed in their spanking new uniforms, into the school pond, which was more akin to a rancid bog than it's grandiose title would suggest, quite why the school provided such a facility for it's bullies still defies explanation, or had suffered the equally unpleasant ritual of having their heads thrust down the toilet bowl whilst an accomplice flushed the chain, if the thugs liked you, or you had anything worth nicking, sometimes they would not shit in the receptacle first. I still get melancholy at the thought of such gratuitous violence and intimidation. Frequently, I read in the papers, how a modern day pupil has hung themselves or slashed their wrists as a result of being bullied at school, today's pupils would not last a minute in the world bullying finals held each year at Maltby Grammar, circa 1972. It was apparent that if I was going to survive my seven year sentence in this den of depravity, I was going to have to wise up pretty fast, as in most jungles this would be a case of survival of the fittest, or possibly the one with the most mates, preferably large ones. I made a mental note to find myself some at the earliest opportunity. My first day at secondary school had not started well, all of the new intake of pupils were ushered into the great hall to be divided into classes and house groups. After the head of year called out each name from the register, the newly formed class would dutifully follow their new form tutor to their designated classrooms/punishment blocks like lambs to the slaughter. I sat through this spectacle and was amazed to discover that there was a pupil in my year with the same surname as myself. This was most unusual, since in eleven years the only other males that I had ever met, who shared my surname, were my father and my uncle. I knew my father had not enlisted in the school ranks because he was at work and my uncle lived too far away, in any case, as far as I was aware, both of them had already completed their education. To intrigue me further, I then discovered that my new found blood relative used my middle name, Russell, as his Christian name. How unusual, I thought, and wondered what the statistical chances of this coincidence occurring would be. Whilst contemplating this strange phenomena I became aware of how empty the hall had become, and became increasingly alarmed to discover that I was the only pupil remaining. I had no class, no house and to make matters worse, I hadn't even had a chance to catch a glimpse of my namesake. I soon discovered why, in my naivety, and partly because I never used my middle name, I had not realised that the head teacher was referring to me when he called out the name Russell Langdale from the register. According to my father I did not have a birth certificate like most people, I had a letter of apology from Durex, I was therefore not in the habit of using my middle name since I didn't even know how to spell it correctly, in truth I only used it on passports, speeding fines and ASBO's. Obviously, the head teacher, who for all his years of experience should have known better, did not make the connection either, even four decades ago the fabric of the education system was already showing signs of fraying around the edges.

I soon discovered that this administrative error had one large plus point or to be more precise two, for some inexplicable reason the head teacher had still not realized his error and as a result I was sent to form 1B, instead of the one allocated. My new form teacher was Miss Slade, why she had chosen a career in education rather than topless modelling or porn movies eluded me, I could easily imagine her in a lead role in 'The Assmaster' or 'Deliveries in the rear, the sequel'. Her name was a total misnomer also, how anybody could ' mislay' such a beauty was incomprehensible, as was the fact that she was perfectly capable of walking upright without constantly falling flat on her nose, such were the size of her finest assets. I compared them, in my mind, to a dead heat in a Zeppelin race, and wondered if her voluminous breasts necessitated the fitting of lead insoles into her shoes to keep her vertical. I made a mental note to buy some tissues on the way home and laminate my textbooks, just to be safe, for sure there would be little point in merely giving them a wrapping of old wallpaper, as instructed by the newly discovered object of my desires.

It was about this time in my formative years that my hormones made their presence felt, I became ever more curious about the opposite sex, especially the one who stood in front of class every morning, like an extra from a Carry On film. Unfortunately, I soon discovered that she was shagging the woodwork teacher, our relationship was doomed from it's inception, he had a flash new TVR sports car, I had the school bus, it just was not going to work. I remember thinking at the time that I hoped his next shit would be a hedgehog, and a large one at that.

I arrived with my fellow pupils, all male since this was pre-equality days, for my first woodwork lesson. Things were so much easier back then, the boys did metalwork or woodwork, the girls did domestic science, where they learned the finer points of baking and were taught how to crochet an orgasm and menstruate quietly.

I duly donned my pristine new apron, which my mother had made, God she knew how to embarrass me, to make matters worse she had 'run up' a track suit from some old crimson material which she had found laying around, ready for my first games lesson, no Nike or Adidas for me it seemed. On reflection, I think I preferred the ways of my primary school, it was less embarrassing with just the old undies and 'music and movement'. However, the beast within was starting to stir, sometimes at the most inopportune moments, which would often cause great personal discomfort, a habit which he continues to this day. With hindsight the more clothes I wore the better, even if I did look like I'd stumbled through the clothes racks of the local 'Help the Aged' shop on a particularly bad day.

The first woodwork lesson involved Romeo the love cheat with the TVR, enlightening his new flock about the dangers of the workshop and familiarizing the class with each of the various tools that adorned the walls. He picked up a plane and announced to the assembled throng, that the blades were extremely sharp and that under no circumstances should they be touched, where upon my new found friend, Perry, promptly proved this to be the case in a most graphic display of blood and stupidity, which resulted in him receiving a clip round the ear from sir and necessitated a trip to the school nurse. Ah, such happy times, I always say 'you can't have too much gratuitous violence in a classroom'.

Perry's mixture of lack of reasoning and ignorance coupled with his mindless stupidity would prepare him well for his future life, he became a police officer. This was in the days when the police had entrance examinations and minimum educational and physical requirements, believe it or not, he was one of the clever ones. It was not sufficient back in the good old days just to be vertically challenged, black, Asian, gay, ginger one legged, female, or preferably a bit of each to get into the force, the prospective applicant had to be intelligent, 'I have no further questions m'Laud, guilty as charged'.

Many years later, I was in the Brewers talking to a regular who knew Perry, coincidentally it turned out that he was a colleague of his and was looking for material for the police magazine, I had recently discovered some old photographs of Perry whilst he was a young probationer, unfortunately for him he was pissed as a fart and mooning at the camera and proudly displaying his bobby's helmet to the world, To the obvious delight of my customer, I furnished him with the negatives, the pictures appeared in the South Yorkshire Police magazine the following month, and were thus circulated to every local station and ultimately it's notice board. Apparently, this caused Perry much personal embarrassment, particularly since he was now the ASBO officer for Rotherham, bloody hypocrite.

He also knew the source of this pornographic filth and was not best pleased that it was now in the public domain. I knew that I would have to ensure my tax disc was up to date from now on, and that I had sufficient funds for bribery purposes, especially when travelling in the vicinity of Rotherham.

I cannot remember many details of my secondary school career. In much the same way as I no longer know how to solve quadratic equations, use logarithms or algebra. To be honest I could not use algebra even in its simplest form in 1977. Likewise, I cannot relate Boyle's law, except the Subo version which states that every woman has the right to be ugly but she is abusing the privilege. I don't give a toss how many wives Henry VIII had or how many King Georges there have been, firstly these facts are not relevant to my daily routine, and secondly our monarchy do not interest me in the slightest, in the same way that my life does not interest them, somehow I can't picture our future King stopping mid polo match to make a telephone call and enquire as to my welfare, it's just a mutual understanding we have, we don't talk about it much, particularly since he married the wizened old tart with the horses head. The only history for which I still have a craving, is modern history, tangible events which have shaped my world since the industrial revolution. It appears that my brain knows that I do not need to remember what I did at 10 am on the 1st December 1974, in the same way that I no longer need to know Pythagoras's theory. Obviously, as I have learned to my detriment, the female mind does not work in this way, discarding obsolete, unused data in order that it can synthesize new data more quickly, in a similar way that a computer operator reformats a hard drive. No, a woman's brain just continues to soak up information like a sponge, ready to be regurgitated at any given time, usually mid-argument, without a doubt, a woman would be able to tell me exactly what she was doing at 10am on the 1st December 1974, moreover she would be able to tell me who she was doing it with, what he was wearing and how late he was, just like a super fast computer chip, if only technology could produce a computer that could clean, cook and play 'hide the sausage', we men would become obsolete overnight and would be able to while away the hours in the local pub watching internet porn and chatting up the barmaid.

I remember the fun that was to be had in the science laboratories, the look of incredulity and bewilderment on the biology masters face upon discovering that some retard had deposited a bottle of concentrated nitric acid into the aquarium, whilst his back was turned, and was now taking side bets on the mortality rate. Or the joys of turning gas taps into flame throwers and the wondrous amusement and sheer horror on a fellow pupils face when he discovered that someone had secretly dropped a burning piece of magnesium ribbon into his new polypropylene blazer pocket, such joy, it's the simple things in life that make it worthwhile.

The school was rightfully proud of its reputation as a seat of learning in the working class mining town and boasted several noted old boys in its bygone registers, Lord Freddie Truman, the Yorkshire and England fast bowler grew up in Maltby, as did Lord Graham Kirkham, known to his friends as 'killer Kirkham' the founder of furniture giant DFS who became a multi millionaire as a result of his endeavours, personally the two noted ex pupils which I remember, as a result of their exploits, remain somewhat less famous, although they nonetheless left their own mark on history. Piggy, thus named as a result of his table manners and personal hygiene techniques, determined to spend the entire length of his secondary school education wearing odd socks, as a result of a ten pence bet with an equally peculiar fellow pupil of the special needs variety, undoubtedly this inane act must have driven his mother mad during laundry time, although, knowing Piggy, he probably didn't bother with such acts of wanton cleanliness, at least his determination and ill-founded stoicism would have prepared him well for his forthcoming career, probably. My second schoolboy hero was a large portly character who, although his exploits and appearance are well remembered, sadly his name is not. He single handedly pioneered unpowered flight for diminutive pet rodents, i.e. hamsters, the technique he developed was to manufacture a small rudimentary parachute from of an old handkerchief and attach a simple harness to each of the four corners, the intrepid fearless aviator was then suspended underneath and promptly oiked out of fat boy's bedroom window to its deserved place in the history books. Whilst animal rights adherents may get hot under their collective collars and subsequently be put off their lentils by such reckless acts, in truth I never once heard the hamster complain whilst it paved the way for rodent aviation. Sadly, our brave aviator died soon after his world record attempt whilst trying to perfect another feat of aerial endurance involving a high level ladder and an ill placed bucket of wallpaper paste in which the poor animal drowned during a late night practice session, whilst fat boy's parents were doing a spot of redecoration.

I recall also the words of my Biology teacher, when he informed me that I would get good results in my A 'level', if only I would attend his classes, rather than boosting the local hostelry's profits. My absence was due to the fact that I had discovered other attractions to occupy my valuable time, most often these attractions were girls and alcohol, or preferably, both together. My tutor had been a member of the old school and was not particularly perturbed by my regular absences, he did however help to instil a love of nature and the living world which I have nurtured ever since, with hindsight it was my love of nature and human biology which would ultimately result in my downfall, although at this stage I was blissfully unaware of this fact.

I could not conceive that knowing how to tell a worms reproductive organs from it's brain or how to dissect a rat's abdomen and be familiar with each part of it's anatomy, would prepare me for the world outside. At no point could I envisage been lost in a giant rat wishing I had paid more attention in class and learned the requisite components and exits of it's body, actually there was one occasion in Yarmouth, but that was self inflicted and chemically induced, Irrespective of how many biology lessons I had attended, I do not think it would have helped that particular situation or placated the arresting officer in any shape, manner or form.

I hated Wednesdays, Wednesdays was quadruple games, a full afternoon of organized torture followed by the melee that was shower time, an altogether loathsome experience. The games master, Mr Moss, was a diminutive character, but that didn't stop him from being a cruel sadistic bastard, who would inflict as much pain as possible on anybody to whom he took a dislike, he could quite easily have been the love child of Caligula and Herman Goering, such was his passion for cruelty. He would derive great joy from making pupils run cross country in the middle of winter, or play the game of organised thuggery which Webb Ellis in his infinite wisdom, decided qualified as a sport, and named it after his location at the time. Perhaps imagination was not one of his strong points, I guess that it was fortuitous that he did not attend Rotherham Technical College, since Saturday afternoons just wouldn't be the same watching a game of Rotherham, instead of Rugby, especially since most of the players would undoubtedly be of Asian origin, on the dole, or both.

I loathed sports with a passion, akin to Saddam Hussain at a Kurd Shoot, it seemed a futile expenditure of my limited energies. It would be much later in my life, about twenty years in fact, before I would savour the joys of long distance running. In my adult years I found it a great escape from life's pressures and somewhat ironically a great way to relax and unwind. My love of running unlike my love of nature was in spite of, and not a result of, my games master. Anyone who has seen the film 'Kes' will make immediate similarities between Brian Glover's character as the bellowing games master and Mr Moss, the only difference being the former was in large screen format. The latter seemed to derive a strange sadistic pleasure from inflicting pain upon his pupils, it seemed he was the sort of person who would pull all the legs off a spider except one, just to watch the unfortunate creature run round in circles, it was not a giant leap of the imagination to envisage him performing the same operation on an unsuspecting eleven year old pupil who had forgotten his games kit.

Mr Moss was usually at his happiest around Easter, this was pre-Bush days when England still had winters, cold ones at that. In his depraved opinion, this was the appropriate time to commence swimming lessons. Not such a daunting ordeal you may think, until being enlightened to the fact that Maltby, at this time, did not have the benefit of an indoor heated pool. Instead it had a small lido situated on 'the crags' some one mile distance from the school, it was unheated, full of leaves and usually had a layer of ice and rat shit on its surface at this time of year, surprisingly even the local population of Polar bears did not venture in until much later in the season. It's Spartan facilities made Auschwitz look like one of Billy Butlins' holiday camps. A more inhospitable place in April would be difficult to find, unless, that is, you were visiting family on Pluto at the time.

The usual routine was that two or three pupils would share a changing cubicle, where they would hurriedly climb into trunks before being unceremoniously thrown into the icy waters for a short course in modern torture techniques, only to discover, upon climbing out, that their dangly bits no longer dangled and their testicles had performed an amazing disappearing double act, only to reappear somewhat sheepishly, some hours later in the maths class, in the relative warmth of the classroom. If that was not an infringement of my human rights, I'll show my prick in Woolie's window, to coin a locally used expression, more often than not it was coined by me, although I cannot claim to be its creator and in no way bear any responsibility for the chain's eventual demise and subsequent bankruptcy.

Strangely, my memory of Maltby Grammar is littered with erroneous and peculiar recollections. On one occasion my statement to my RE teacher, who had foolishly enquired as to what his pupils knew about Damascus, was that I had heard that it killed 99% of household germs. The teacher had been from the old school, when he had proper pupils to teach and hence did not find my witty retort in the slightest degree humorous, he did not take kindly to my insubordination and obvious lack of respect for all things religious, this resulted in a long wait outside the headmasters office, and a short course in pain via the extremities of his cane. In the modern world this obviously would no longer be allowed, although I still know people who will gladly part with hard earned money to endure such suffering.

One of many of my school days, which I can still recall, was meeting the author Barry Hines, a talented writer from Barnsley who wrote the highly acclaimed 'Kes'. He wrote in an every day style with which I was familiar, he was also infinitely more interesting than Chaucer, Beowulf and Shakespeare, all of whose works I was required to study for 'O' level English Literature, and all of which bored the proverbial arse off me. This is probably the reason why it was the only exam I ever failed, it bored me rigid, and in truth I would rather have hammered nails into my eye sockets than read another chapter of Macbeth. The only pleasure to be derived from the lesson was seeing how far I could wind up the tutor. I had christened her 'Egor', since she had, deservedly in my humble opinion, suffered from a thyroid condition and had a large scar across her neck, all that was missing to complete the picture was a large bolt through her skull, which I would have obligingly implanted if asked nicely ,children can be so cruel. I had a loathing and healthy disrespect for her, and could tell that the feeling was mutual. In hindsight, she bore more than a passing similarity to a portly Edwina Currie in her later years, although I doubt if Egor had ever been the benefactor of the carnal delights of the inside of John Major's underpants.

Another encounter I would not forget, was an afternoon in the presence of Group Captain Sir Douglas Bader CBE who, despite the loss of both legs in a flying accident, still managed to down 22 German planes in World War II, before being shot down and taken prisoner. Even then, he still proved to be a thorn in the German's side with his numerous escape attempts, which resulted in the German's sending him to the 'escape proof' Colditz Castle and threatening to confiscate his artificial legs. Such was the German's respect for the man, that when he lost one of his artificial legs whilst bailing out of his stricken spitfire they allowed the RAF safe passage to St Omer, a Luftwaffe base to drop off a replacement. Apparently, they were really pissed off when, after completing the delivery the large armada of bombers and fighter escorts went on to bomb the power station at Gosnay, cheeky bastards!

As my school career progressed, my friendship with a couple of older pupils flourished, they had been a couple in the biblical sense, for several years, and took me under their collective wings. They will for reasons which will become readily apparent, remain nameless. On reflection, I did not realise at the time, that I was being groomed for their sexual gratification, in my naïve way I just thought they were being friendly, at least that's what I told the judge. I would not realise the full implications of their actions until a, few years later when they had married and bought a house of their own. They would buy me presents and keep me in gin and beer, I would do the many DIY jobs around the house and garden, I was good at that sort of thing, and it was a pleasant release from the routine adolescent boredom of picking spots and masturbating, although, not necessarily at the same time.

Some mornings we would drive at sunrise to the nearby Clumber Park, a National Trust forest some twenty five miles away, in their new pride and joy, a 1300cc vermillion coloured Austin Allegro. At the time I thought it was the dogs bollocks, not that my opinion on anything involving an engine at the time was worth a jot, since I also thought his dad's two litre Austin Princess was pretty snazzy. Oh, the shame of it all, I've kept that secret bottled up for all these years. What were the designers of this masterpiece of British engineering thinking of when they furnished the Allegro with a square steering wheel, was it a Friday afternoon afterthought, no doubt precipitated by the fact that it was POETS day? For thousands of years, man had been the benefactor of the invention of the wheel, it's design had been honed and strengthened over the decades, but it was still essentially a wheel, round at all corners.

I could picture the scene in ancient Egypt in the court of the great pharaoh Ramesis II, upon being presented with a fabulous new chariot, it's golden panels glistening in the afternoon sun, before it a magnificent team of immaculately groomed white horses, only to find on it's inaugural journey that it's ride was less than smooth and accompanied by a somewhat unnerving thud, thud, thud. I could envisage the incredulous expression on the pharaoh's face, upon discovering that some clown had fitted a bespoke pair of square wheels to his new mode of transport. It would be little use the carpenter explaining to the boss, that he thought his decision would negate the fitting of a handbrake. If only Austin-Rover had spent their time solving the riddle of why their products miraculously turned into a pile of rust the moment they left the factory, instead of trying to reinvent the wheel, they would probably still be in business today.

My friends had done well for themselves, she had a good job as a civil servant, he worked in the bank and would later become the manager, they had successfully climbed the social ladder and become respected members of society. To my twisted way of thinking all this served to make the following events, all the more bizarre. One night after copious amounts of the falling down juice, the three of us finished up in the same bed, fortunately, it was a king size, for she was a large girl, approximately as broad as she was tall, my was she tall, she could well have been the product of a one night stand between Hattie Jaques, to whom she bore more than a passing resemblance, and the Russian Olympic shot put team. If the bed in question had been a water bed, I would doubtlessly still be riding the bow wash and would consequently be feeling very sea sick. Coincidentally, this was pretty much how I did feel, not because I had spontaneously developed morals, but for two simple reasons. Firstly, I had never before, or thankfully since, had sexual encounters with a whale, David Attenborough and Greenpeace would be furious, I could picture them with buckets of water, in a vain attempt to keep the beast moist until the arrival of the next high tide. Secondly, I have never performed such intimate manoeuvres whilst being closely scrutinized by the recipients partner, it must have been like watching a television wildlife programme, in which I played the leading role, David Bellamy would have been proud of me. I could picture his narrative to accompany the film 'Here we have the seldom seen but often heard, Homus Nobbus Langdalus, in his natural habitat, a bedroom. After a protracted courtship ritual involving the green offerings called Gordon's to the female, which festoon the mating chamber floor, the actual copulation is completed in a surprisingly short time. The male then plays no further part in the relationship'. I could not, however, envisage how he was going to explain to the assembled masses watching their televisions at home, the presence of the female's bank manager husband in his sometimes all too proximate observational capacity to my wedding tackle. To this day I have never been totally convinced as to either his motives for this evidently pre-planned sojourn to Hades, nor his sexuality. I had often wondered if he was a friend of Mary's, who frequently got off the other bus to do a little uphill gardening around the back passage. Minutes earlier, I was wondering, with no small amount of trepidation, if I was to be used as a human condom, the filling in a debauched sandwich, replete with an over zealous helping of man mayonnaise. I had hoped that our alliance would assist me in receiving a cheap mortgage, but instead, as with most things of a banking nature, the instant I made a withdrawal, I immediately lost interest. I promised myself that never again would I sleep with any woman who was capable of devouring her own body weight in after eight mints, and whose idea of a romantic night in was a plate of dripping sandwiches, a case of Guinness and Coronation Street.

Towards the twilight of my education, the powers that were decided that each pupil should have a counselling session with the careers master. This towering figure looked like an extra from a Boris Carloff horror film. Since I had never had the slightest inkling as to what my chosen vocation in life was going to be, this meeting only served to give me grounding in interview techniques for any future meetings with a Relate counsellor. He duly asked me what I was going to do upon leaving school. I hurriedly contemplated my options, professional sausage knotter, bespoke sock darner, self-employed pencil sharpener, none of them would stretch my abilities. I replied that I had been seriously considering training to become a pair of curtains, where upon I was rapidly ushered out of the door, that Billy Elliot had life so easy compared to me!

With hindsight, I wished that I had told him that I wanted to be an intrepid explorer like Ranolph Fiennes or Ellen McCarthur, just to see the look on his face. After due consideration he might have reasoned that to many people this statement would have been more ridiculous than my initial reply. How do these people get the funding to shoot off around the world on adventure holidays, how do they get the time off work, who feeds the dog whilst they are away? Certainly, most of us lesser mortals would love to disappear to some uninhabited island paradise, in some far off ocean and do fuck all for the duration, but we are all too busy doing proper jobs, get a life you spoilt bastards.

I left Maltby Grammar school some weeks later, surprisingly I had accumulated more than an average bag of qualifications, I would have obtained more if I had not developed the habit of popping down to the local at lunchtime with the teachers, for a pint or two, and fingering the head girl behind the stage. Despite my new found enlightenment my career opportunities were about as inviting as a three legged veal calf in a recession, since my parents kindly informed me that I could either seek employment down the local mine courtesy of the NCB, or seek gainful remuneration via the steelworks, the alternative, apparently, was to seek sanctuary in someone else's residence, I had learned the meaning of the word 'heartache', my girlfriend had eloped with my best mate, I did miss him! They were later to marry and continue to be contented and good friends of mine, a point which was strangely lost on my wife, who likely as not, watched the David Bellamy series in the late 70's and feared a remake of episode two. The only other memories I left this bastion of the education system with, were a love of music, an intimate knowledge of the pertinent parts of the female form and a strangely irritating rash, still, I had mastered the technique of retrieving a rubber brick from the bottom of a swimming pool whilst wearing my pyjamas and was able to cycle proficiently, happy days,

Thailand

Knicker Dave was a large man, he had been carrying John Smiths beer baby since long before our first meeting, a fact which made an elephant's gestation period seem brief. I first met him as a customer in the Brewers, where he would regularly adulterate a fine stout with copious amounts of vintage port, he was Mansfield's gold medal winning heathen. As he frequently pointed out, Dave didn't have a drink problem, he knew he could get one any time of the day or night. Indeed, on market days, he had perfected the art of waking me at 7.30am with a piercing whistle, from beneath my bedroom window, in order that he could start his day with a 'swift snifter'. Occasionally, when he was feeling kind to his liver, Dave would have a day off the beer and drink coke instead, usually accompanied by several large vodkas, thus he had earned his other nickname, 'Topshelf Trussy', he was careful with his health that way. His body had been a temple, now it resembled a god, Buddha, if he had been any more laid back, he would have been horizontal or would have disappeared up his own anus years ago like an over exuberant arse gymnast. He reminded me of an ageing Lou Feringou on Prozac, although I never actually saw him turn green, surprising really considering the things Dave threw down his throat. Dave had a wicked sense of humour and loved to be the centre of attraction, unusually this did not impede our friendship, since this was usually my job. With Dave I didn't object to a bit of job sharing, although we never took the time to write a formal contract, we shared the work and made a pretty good double act. Dave, and for that matter Paula his long suffering wife, were into knickers in a big way. For thirty years they had been market traders in the lingerie business. I could picture the look on Dave's career teacher's face when he informed him that, in his opinion, his chosen vocation would involve getting into knickers, whereupon his adviser would probably suggest that he should become a pair of curtains instead!

Dave was an accomplished trombone and French horn player, this was quite a remarkable achievement, since in 57 years on the planet, he had never owned an instrument. Instead he had diligently whiled away the hours practising with just his lips, apparently the instruments were superfluous and a waste of hard earned beer coupons. Dave was a veritable walking brass section, interestingly, he played by ear, unlike his peers he had dispensed with sheet music altogether. His warm up piece was a sublime rendition of a 55 Deltic's two tone horn, this always went down well in a crowded restaurant after a few 'snifters'.

Every year for the past decade Dave and Paula had avoided the British winters and escaped to Thailand for a few months respite care. When they asked if I fancied joining them my answer was forthcoming in a nanosecond, 'too bloody right I did, do bears shit in the woods?, do big dogs fart?' France had been a welcome relief from the chaos that had become my life, although it had only been a few weeks previous it felt like years. The pressure had been growing to make some life changing decisions since my return, like a giant carbuncle my life was going to burst and make one hell of a mess along the way. I reasoned that two months seclusion 6000 miles away from the UK would give my wife and girlfriend, not to mention myself, some valuable thinking time, and would hopefully help to solve some of the problems that were by now all too apparent, my percussion lessons at Braithwell County Primary School had not given me sufficient grounding to play this particular triangle in anything other than a very amateur and pathetic way. I figured that my job offer from the London Philharmonic would not be dropping through my letter box in the foreseeable future, and that the most prudent course of action was to run away as quickly as possible.

Early January saw Dave, Paula and myself negotiating the concourse of the new Bangkok airport, after the long flight from Manchester via Abu Dhabi. Our introduction to Thailand was less than ideal, and would even try the patience of the usually recumbent Dave. After a half mile trek down the unfeasibly long arrivals lounge, we asked the staff at the information desk if it was necessary to report to passport control for the impending flight to Koh Samui, our island destination in the gulf of Thailand, or if like our baggage, we were cleared for the next flight. To our amazement the young girl informed us that this was not necessary and that we should make our way, a further half mile, to the check-in desk for Bangkok Air, this was not the slow and inefficient service of which I had been told, my elation however was short lived.

The departure hall was busier than Gainsborough post office on giro day, everywhere there were queues, we asked the young smartly dressed assistant which queue we should join, since that was her job, she would obviously know, heaven forbid we would wait in the wrong queue. She didn't and we did, on reaching the desk some one hour of queuing later, as instructed, we were directed to the adjacent queue. By this time I was becoming extremely bored with the whole game, to my mind there is only a certain amount of fun to be had staring at a fellow travellers back. Incredibly, after a further thirty minute wait, we reached the desk, only to be informed that we should have cleared passport control previously and could not board the plane without the requisite paperwork. Next time, I reasoned, I was going to travel inside my suitcase, firstly there was more legroom than on the Boeing 777, peasant class, in which I had spent the best part of a day practicing my cramped sardine impression, and secondly, unlike myself, my suitcase had made the transition to the cargo hold of the connecting plane relatively easily, a fact which to this day still amazes me.

In order to obtain the paperwork we had to hurriedly walk the mile back to passport control, where we were given a long and protracted demonstration of the supermarket queue syndrome. After being unceremoniously ushered into a designated line of fellow travellers, the unfortunate spectator is required to stand and watch helplessly as every other queue moves at ten times the speed of their own. This situation was exacerbated by the fact that the security guard, who like most of his colleagues spoke less English than I spoke Thai, i.e. none, insisted on moving everybody except myself and my companions from the queues behind to the faster moving ones, at this rate it was obvious that we would miss our connecting flight. A further thirty minute queue awaited on the fourth floor, where for the third time, we attempted to check-in. We had found the desk more by accident than design, as stated most of the staff were not familiar with the intricacies of the English language, furthermore the management apparently wished to keep the location of the domestic departure desks a closely guarded secret, from both their staff and their customers.

Eventually, after a further one mile walk, we were ushered onto the plane, an ageing Boeing, which despite the colourful mural that adorned the fuselage, could not hide the fact that it had only recently been fitted with pneumatic tyres and could easily have been a veteran of the Iwo Jima campaign. Quite definitely it belonged in a museum, it didn't exactly have an outside toilet but it wasn't that far off, if it had it would doubtlessly have been furnished with a roll of Izal Shiny. Since writing this I have returned to Koh Samui only to discover that this relic of aviation had given up the ghost and had subsequently crashed on landing and what remains of it is now deposited in a sorry state at the end of the runway in an ungainly reminder of a bygone era of steam powered aviation history.

'I spy with my little eye, something beginning with LR' I quipped to Dave as we climbed the steps to the plane, the blank expression on his face apparently required an answer. 'Loose rivet', I giggled in my inimitable childish manner, Paula, in the timeless words of Procul Harum turned a whiter shade of pale and promptly shat herself.

If the obvious age of our aircraft was not sufficient to induce more than a little sphincter trembling, the ten year old in uniform, who was making his way towards the cockpit with a booster cushion under one arm and a flight plan under the other, certainly was. Our pilot made the French gendarmerie look positively geriatric, in order to obtain his flying qualifications I guessed that he must have had a flight simulator implanted in his mother's womb, I wondered if she would be angry if he wasn't home in time for his favourite tea, alpha-betti noodles on toast and lashings of ginger beer, no doubt.

Koh Samui's airport is like no other I have ever encountered, it consists of a couple of open sided huts, thatched with coconut leaves, or terminal one and two, as they are somewhat optimistically titled. Arriving passengers are ferried from the steps of the plane to the terminal, on what can only be described as a horse drawn tram without the horse, actually it did have a couple of horses under the floor, confined in a very noisy smoking engine, which was possibly salvaged from one of Henry Fords prototypes, judging by the noise they were doing their utmost to escape. The driver steered by means of a tiller and, like myself, had no idea where the brakes were, if indeed there were any. This small oversight did not stop the convoy of dilapidated milk floats from racing along the perimeter of the airfield to win the first to the arrivals lounge, aka hut number three, trophy, like a bungled start of the 2.30 at Chepstow.

Dave's friend Trev had arranged to meet us at the airport, surprisingly he was nowhere to be seen, fortunately he had sent another friend to greet us, due in no small part to the fact that Trev had decided that he would take the opportunity to have a massive heart attack, and as a result was lying in a hospital bed in Bangkok, the selfish bastard, Dave said with Trev it was always a case of me, me, me. I wondered if he had suffered similar problems as ourselves when he checked in to the hospital A and E department, if so he would no doubt by now be dead following a protracted tour via the GU medicine, antenatal, paediatrics and kitchen department, before being finally directed towards coronary care. Fortunately for Trev, he had obviously upgraded to 'club class' and survived his ordeal.

In contrast to the air-conditioned environment of the previous twenty four hours, Thailand was hot and humid, as were my pair of Marks and Spencer's finest, which had had far too much time during the flight to become intimate with the contours of my nether region's protuberances and crevices.

I had left behind the gales and snows which were ravaging Britain and now the perspiration was dripping off my forehead, with hindsight maybe the sheepskin coat was a slight error of judgement on my behalf, as usual my sartorial elegance left a lot to be desired.

Our jeep was waiting at the airport, puddle number three, mud park one. Within ten minutes I was ensconced in my new residence, a brand new, air conditioned bungalow surrounded by coconut trees and banana palms.

Following the restrictions of the journey, it was good to stretch my legs and discover my new surroundings. The first thing I noticed were the houses of the local people, they were the simplest I have ever seen. In truth, they were little more than a raised dais with a corrugated iron roof and bamboo walls, it appeared that the local building inspector had the easiest job in town. The furniture usually consisted of a mattress on the floor, a wide screen television and a cooling fan, these people took the minimalist style of architecture to another level. The little shacks appeared more incongruous since they were dotted between more modern opulent holiday homes, hotels and houses of the more wealthy residents. The king of Thailand had been on the throne for over sixty years, perhaps this was a consequence of drinking the local water or eating too many green curries, in either case the fact apparently entitled him to the title of the world's longest reigning monarch. To celebrate this milestone, he decreed that each house should have an unfeasibly large satellite dish that would make Jodrell Bank look diminutive, at all times this must be tuned to a British Football match. Furthermore, each house must have an equally enormous 4x4 pick up truck parked outside. I figured that American Express must have had one hell of a sales drive recently, I could not envisage any other way that these people could afford such trimmings of opulence short of selling the odd Kidney or two, no wonder they lived in huts. It appeared that the Thai people didn't have much in the way of chattels but at least they had their priorities right. I have grafted for the best part of thirty years and am still unable to afford either of these luxuries, indeed I haven't even got as far as owning a television set, preferring as I do, to gawp at Dixon's display window for a weekly treat, alas they switch the TVs off before Babe station starts transmission.

The poor unfortunates who were still awaiting the delivery of their new turbocharged, leather clad, air-conditioned pimpmobiles in the meantime had to make do with a moped. In the

UK this would have seriously impeded family transport, but not in Thailand, they used them to transport everything be it giant sacks and bales of recycled plastic bottles or cardboard boxes, shopping, dogs, parcels, a family of four and it's pet gecko, in fact anything. Furthermore, the fact that they were on two wheels did not stop them from smoking a cigarette, using their mobile phones or having a conversation with the dog, sometimes they would perform all three operations at the same time. Once on a visit to Panjim in India, I had observed a man travelling on a similar moped carrying a fifty foot scaffolding pole over his shoulder, just to make this wondrous feat more interesting he had determined to perform this act of lunacy during rush hour on a four lane highway. I truly believed that I would never see the exploits of this nutter bettered in the entertainment stakes. I was wrong. In Thailand it is apparently acceptable to carry a whole bundle of bamboo scaffolding poles of a similar length on a moped, the only difference to the previous incumbent being that this one carried the poles in a sideways, as opposed to an inline, manner. Certainly at this rate, it would not be very long before the rider graphically demonstrated the basics of Darwin's theories of evolution and went to talk to the worms.

Apparently, age was not an important factor in deciding who could, or could not ride a moped, as I walked along the roadside I was amazed to see a boy of no more than seven or eight carrying a passenger several years his junior, very rarely did the riders employ crash helmets or suitable footwear, they simply trundled along in a pair of shorts and flip flops, the only item of safety wear I ever witnessed being utilised was a dust mask.

If the man transporting the bamboo poles seemed ridiculous, the three men in the pick up truck dragging an entire tree behind the vehicle, down the main road of Chong Mong, was totally sublime, at least the road was well swept. I could only guess what they intended to do with the tree upon reaching their destination, if indeed they ever did. Strange that in India, as in Thailand, even in the busy towns with such peculiar driving techniques, I never once witnessed any anger or malice between fellow drivers, not even a hint of road rage. How very different to our western culture, I use the term in it's loosest context.

I had noticed the vast array of electricity cables which festooned the posts along the roadsides, they were draped like enormous strands of spaghetti hung out to dry. At regular intervals this overhead macramé was bundled together with a piece of old twine, as I turned the corner my attention was arrested by a group of electrical contractors who were working on the power lines, not a hard hat in sight. Each of them was resplendent in T-shirts, shorts and flip flops, their only tools were apparently a pair of old pliers, some string and step ladders. The man hanging from the wires was apparently attempting to splice in a new cable, as if there were not sufficient already, it was as if every electrical appliance on the island had it's own dedicated wire running directly from the power station. Just to make the splicing operation a little more dangerous it had started to rain.

Since I had been raised in the UK, an island not renowned for it's arid climate, I reasoned that I knew a thing or two about rain. I was wrong, my knowledge of the subject was indeed very limited. I had never experienced a deluge like the one in which I now found myself, the giant raindrops were being thrown from on high with incredible force and in such large quantities, it was obvious that St Peter and his work force in the heaven factory had been on one almighty lager bender the night before. The showers back home had not prepared me for this cataclysmic display of mother nature's power. If rain was football this was a premiership performance, the UK was still wallowing at the bottom of the conference league.

Along the roadside each tiny homestead was supported by the family business which was usually located at the front of the property by the road. On a desolate area of ground I watched the local drain maker as he handcrafted three feet diameter concrete drain sections in moulds. He was wearing the standard uniform, the obligatory T-shirt and flip flops. His business was evidently booming since the local authorities had decided to install a new main drain to prevent the flooding of previous years, judging by the number of completed sections which were drying in the sun, trade was brisk, although I could not see the company floating on the stock exchange in the immediate future. Next door a couple owned a small stall selling fruit and vegetables, they were sat cross legged on the floor and were busy breaking large pieces of charcoal into smaller ones, before packaging the pieces into small plastic bags for resale, they had dispensed with T-shirts but were still wearing the compulsory flip flops, their lack of shirts was probably explained by the fact that they were covered from head to toe in thick black charcoal dust, I expected at any moment that they would break into an Al Jolson rendition from the Jazz Singer.

At regular intervals along the way were motor bike repair garages, these tin shacks were kept busy from morning until late at night. In part they were busy because of the large numbers of mopeds on the islands roads and partly because there was no word in Thai language for fast, probably. They have one speed, pedestrian, it takes them a week to do a days job. The average wage in Thailand is approximately fifteen pounds a week, to the casual observer this figure probably appears to be on the low side, in truth if the workers were paid commensurate to the amount of work undertaken this figure would be significantly reduced. This, I reasoned, is why the airport staff were so inept, they were paid a pittance because that is all they deserved and thus they were about as much use as a chocolate fireguard. Not that this fact in anyway detracted from their happiness, time was someone else's concept, they had bundles of it and were going nowhere in a similar way to a 'Chelsea Tractor' on the M25 during Friday night rush hour, circa 6pm.

If the Thai's had to wait three days for a parking space in the car park of the local Tesco's it didn't matter, they weren't doing anything else, there was always tomorrow, this was one possible explanation why they did not lose their tempers when behind the steering wheels of their vehicles.

To my amazement the mechanics in the garages not only used welding tackle whilst wearing their flip flops, but they had also dispensed with any form of face mask or eye protection. I figured the local health and safety inspector had been made redundant years ago and was probably a travelling flip flop salesman by now. Perhaps it was his suggestion that the workers should, at the very least, wear steel toe capped sandals and flame retardant T-shirts that finally tipped the balance and resulted in his inevitable demise. Perhaps it was the sight of the method of fuel dispense at these garages which ultimately resulted in him being sectioned and spending the remainder of his life in a warm little cell with very soft wall paper, whilst wearing strange designer jackets, minus sleeves and fastened up the back, that eventually led to his untimely breakdown. Each of the garages had a small covered stall from which they sold the fuel, this was pumped by hand from adjacent forty gallon drums into a transparent reservoir, where it was measured and dispensed. Since some of the fuel was yellow and some red, the fuel stations resembled cocktail bars, it was easy to picture a prospective customer asking for a cherry octane bomb or a banana shake. The less safety conscious garage proprietors had dispensed with all this fancy technical modern wizardry, preferring instead to sell the fuel in second hand wine bottles, complete with corks, for thirty Bahts a throw. The bottles were then lined up along the bar in thirty plus degrees of mid-day sun, to await customers, these bottles were filled from plastic receptacles via the use of a funnel. Amazingly I witnessed one owner performing this task with a cigarette hanging from the corner of his mouth, I imagine by now he is probably the only person selling fuel in lower earth orbit. At least the bizarre and potentially lethal exploits of the fuel merchants provided me with hours of entertainment, a trip to fill up was so much more exciting than at home, I fully expected, with each subsequent visit to the local bomb factory, to find a sign informing customers that it was now compulsory to smoke and use mobile phones whilst filling up!!

Every inch of roadside space was utilized in some way or another, those traders who could not afford premises plied their trade on foot. The knife salesman carried a bamboo bag over his shoulder, this was full of knives and no doubt represented his entire stock. The brush salesman had a small hand cart on which he displayed his collection of grass and bamboo brushes whilst parading the streets. One woman sold cheap jewellery fashioned from sea shells and coconuts, she displayed her wares via a stick across her shoulders, whilst she was walking. I witnessed her answer her mobile phone, I guessed she was possibly checking the closing figures of the Dow Jones Index, in reality she was probably being informed that her husband had just left her, and indeed every other inhabitant of planet earth, following an explosion at the local filling station.

Some of the more ambitious entrepreneurs had fitted sidecars fashioned from angle iron and old toasters to their mopeds, this provided them with a mobile retail outlet. Although the resultant contraption had the appearance of a sale item from the Thai division of Messer's Heath and Robinson, it meant that the owner could transport and sell his wares to a larger market. This they did for hours on end, they sold everything from freshly made sweet smelling pancakes which were fashioned on the spot and served with a selection of sauces for 30 baht, the equivalent of 40 pence, to spicy Tom yum soup with noodles and crispy pork and dumplings.

These vehicles were used for a wide variety of purposes, as I walked to the beach, I had a peculiar vision, I watched the couple equipped with brush and shovel astride their bike/trailer combination. They wore face masks and rubber gloves, I guessed that they were either exponents of a new sexual fetish which I had not yet read about in 'fetishing weekly', or they were street cleaners, I chose the latter. Not only did this couple clean the streets and empty the bins but they also rummaged through the sacks of rotting rubbish for plastic bottles and cardboard, for which they would receive money at the recycling plant, the strangest thing was that they carried out their duties whilst wearing red and white Xmas bobble hats with a sprig of holly on the front which appeared totally incongruous in thirty plus degrees. Many of the roadside collection bins were fashioned from old tyres, these were cut, turned inside out and riveted together, complete with lid and a stand made from motorcycle tyres, they looked like giant cauldrons, the Thai's were obviously adherents to the rule of waste not want not.

Unlike in the UK, these bins were not emptied every two weeks, but on a daily basis, the system allowed for recycling without the need for micro chipped bins and an army of health and safety box ticking gurus, there were no threats of government intervention and extra taxes for the poor unfortunate who had inadvertently placed an empty wine bottle in the wrong bin, the Thai's just got on with the job in hand, they were undoubtedly one of the most polite and honest people I have ever encountered and appeared to be content with their lot. I reasoned that a job exchange programme with the pen pushing parasites of Team GB's local government offices would not go a miss and might even result in some form of efficiency, not that I intended to hold my breath on that score The Thai psyche is such that even when they have a military coup no shots are fired, they just quietly change jobs, have a cup of tea and give the population an extra day off, in Thailand I repeatedly found myself asking the question 'who was right and who was wrong', usually, in my opinion, it was the western world that was the latter. Despite the sun rising at around 5.30am even the cockerels that lived in the trees around the bungalow had developed this laid back attitude, if they could be bothered at all they started to crow at around mid-day, by which time their European counterparts would have long since shut up shop, clocked off and been ready to hit the town. As with most markets, the market in Bangrak was a noisy bustling place, the fish market in particular entertained me for hours. Each stall was a banquet of giant prawns, cuttlefish, octopus, mussels, bright blue crabs with their claws tied together, small clams which were eaten raw like baby oysters with a sweet chilli dipping sauce, fish of every size, colour and state of decomposition and preservation, red snapper, mackerel, shark, barracuda all glistened on beds of ice in the morning freshness, the aromas filled the sea air. Each stall had a system of small electric motors hung above it's wares, these revolved wire and handkerchief contraptions, in a helicopter like fashion, and thus deterred the flies from acquiring a free lunch, although they did give the appearance of an out of time and inebriated troop of 'Morris dancers'. After the stall holders and roadside traders closed for the day, they simply covered their wares with a plastic sheet or rolled down a tarpaulin from the roof, if the stall had one, such was the honesty of the population that theft was obviously not a problem, I imagined the market traders of Gainsborough employing this method of stock rotation on a Friday night, by Saturday morning they would be lucky if the stall was still there, not to mention it's contents. I witnessed a similar display of honesty in action at the local branch of Tesco, a shopper had completed the days task and parked the trolley which was full of groceries outside the KFC, I pondered for a while, firstly why would anybody wish to eat at KFC when they were surrounded by incredibly cheap and excellent fresh local food and, secondly how long would a similar trolley and contents remain outside the KFC branch in Meadowhall, Sheffield? Probably marginally longer than the CD player in the owner's car in the car park.

I reasoned that these public displays of honesty were probably an offshoot of the population's deep rooted Buddhist beliefs, that and the fact that any serious transgression was likely to lead to a rapid and violent execution. Every where in Thailand is the face of Buddhism, every bar, restaurant, shop and house has a shrine where each day offerings of food and drink are made. On one occasion in a local beach shack I saw the modern face of Buddhism when the young staff diligently made an offering of three 'Dunkin Donuts', from a large box purchased that morning, and a Fanta orange juice, talk about trendy modern idols and religious evolution.

Each property had in it's garden a brightly decorated prayer shrine, these constructions stood approximately six feet tall and were painted in bright reds, turquoise and gold. My initial assumption, on seeing them for the first time, was that they were the most elaborate bird tables I had ever seen, they even had fairy lights to aid the owls with their night time manoeuvres. However, closer inspection revealed that they were adorned with joss sticks and prayer offerings which were sacrosanct and integral to the owner's beliefs. I reflected that if I had a similar construction in my front garden it would rapidly be full of the holy offerings of fag packets and beer cans, together with that most sacred of gifts, second hand chewing gum, such was the devotion of my local congregation, realistically, within twenty four hours, it would probably be in transit to the local car boot sale.

I pulled up a stool at the bar of the small thatched shack, lit my pipe and was about to drink breakfast, that being the day's first bottle of Singha beer, when the morning peace was shattered, one hundred feet above my head, by the Boeing's engines. The bar was located at the end of the islands runway and directly beneath the flight path, consequently, every half an hour, I was made to feel like an extra from Apocalypse Now, At the time I was quietly contemplating the fact that, unlike in France and despite the large number of dogs on the island, there was a total absence of calling cards. During my entire stay there was only one occasion when I happened across a solitary canine nest, resplendent with it's clutch of freshly laid 'dog eggs' waiting to hatch, it was obvious that Koh Samui would not be the best starting point for the avid seeker of the almost extinct albino dog log. Suddenly my unorthodox thought patterns were interrupted by an altogether more pressing and potentially more serious cerebral musing. I had travelled 6000 miles to decide my future and draw some lines under my past, in so doing I had been transported to the biggest den of iniquity on the planet where the pursuance of sin is compulsory and celibacy is a criminal offence, probably. Necessity had dictated that I was going to abstain from any pleasures of the flesh for two very long months, I felt like an orphaned child in a Charles Dickens Christmas story who had been taken on a shopping trip to Toys R Us by Mr Scrooge, there was no way that I was going to get to play with any of the toys on show. The last time I achieved such a momentous feat I was a foetus and was still more than a little reluctant to leave. The task was made more difficult since I was surrounded by slim, beautiful women who all looked fifteen years old, even their grandmothers would have been more than acceptable after a couple of Singhas, it wasn't even necessary to close one eye and squint a little. I determined that I would possibly have to risk the sight of one eye and allow Madam Palm and her five lovely daughters to shake the sticky white fruits from the tree of love, the only other alternative was self operation of the single action yoghurt pump. I reasoned that my life was complicated enough already, and thus in the pursuit of sanity, I would not be availing myself of the local talent, better to go blind than risk being emasculated with a blunt razor blade on my return home, I reasoned.

Gradually, I became aware that the bar girls were a little more friendly and tactile than was customary, this was also true of the assembled group of leather clad tattooed bikers who arrived on their 50cc monsters and ordered a round of Babychams. Inadvertently I had stumbled across the only gay bar on the island, it transpired that a large proportion of the staff were 'Kathoey' or to put it in 'farang'(westerner) terms, ladyboys, albeit very attractive ones. It should have been obvious when I arrived, members of the opposite sex, not to mention my own, do not normally fall over themselves to get to me in such a manner, nor do they usually have Adam's apples which are larger than their breasts. At this point my resolve to remain celibate strengthened, it would be just my luck to discover at the moment of truth that my new found bed guest had an extra portion of meat and two vegetables. I determined that if I did find myself in such a situation the obligatory Crocodile Dundee handshake would be indispensable, somehow I could not envisage myself at the Magnus Magnusson old boy's school reunion uttering the words 'I started so I finished', moreover I had no ardent desires to become the sex kitten of the local biker's posse, I finished my beer and made my excuses.

If Chong Mong was a quiet backwater, Lamai was positively vibrant, I arrived stood astride the rear of the jeep like a modern day Boadicea without the horses, from this vantage point it was easier to see, hear and smell my surroundings in greater detail. I could not comprehend why the Thai's needed television, there was so much to observe. The streets throbbed with shops, bars, roadside BBQ's, traders of every imaginable ware, barbers and hyperbaric chambers, these were an offshoot of the excellent local diving available, although their presence did seem a little incongruous in such humble surroundings. It was midnight and Lamai was buzzing, the humid night air was filled with the scent of jasmine and baby oil, every bar pumped out ear splitting music, the town was one big party where the only thing that was taboo was having morals. The streets were lined with numerous 'Girly Bars', where the prospective customer was virtually dragged in by the slim young sex engineers, at least that was my excuse for conducting a little investigative journalism. I eyed the frontage of the imaginatively named 'Beaver Bar' and considered the relative merits of employing similar methods to achieve customer satisfaction in the Brewers, eventually common sense prevailed, I postulated that certain members of the staff were not fully up to speed with this kind of customer liaison and would require a refresher course or two, not to mention a whole series of injections and surgical procedures.

I removed the girls eager hand from down the front of my jeans and suggested that we should play a game of pool instead, my lack of training in such situations dictated that I should be a student of the 'play hard to get' school of thought. Unfortunately, I hadn't counted on two pertinent points, firstly to these young sex technicians, time was money and secondly, as a result of spending so much time in the bars, the girls were excellent pool masters. My excuse for allowing myself to be so comprehensively embarrassed was that I had never played on a table with bunkers before, such was the state of the cloth, the reality of the situation was that there were too many distractions surrounding me to concentrate on a futile game of pool, especially since my opponent was apparently more used to a set of balls banging on her chin rather than into a pocket on a pool table. I scrutinized the bar's other victims as they were parted from their hard earned cash, there wasn't exactly a 'girl' menu on the wall but the customers appeared to know what was available. In a similar sales pitch to the neighbouring restaurants, the customer could select the evenings choice from the display at the front of the premises, the only difference seemed to be that this catch of the day was not in a fridge, in contrast the evenings selection was red hot! The next decision which the customer was required to make was whether he wanted 'short time, or 'long time', this was a relatively easy decision that was some what akin to paying for car parking facilities. 'Short time', as it's name suggested, usually involved a sprint finish in a nearby room, shack or backseat, where as 'long time' was for the more seasoned long distance athletes and usually entailed an all night training session in a nearby hotel. After selecting the lucky recipient and paying the 'bar fine', a somewhat poetic nomenclature for protection money to the pimp who owned the bar, it was simply a case of a moped ride to Shagsville for a quick game of Mr Wobbly hides his helmet. For less than ten pounds, it was apparently possible to achieve a basic grounding in debauchery and a more extensive knowledge of various weird and colourful exotic diseases and knob viruses, to be fair these girls could make Chlamydia sound like a beautiful island retreat in the Maldives.

In Thailand prostitution together with the antics of the ladyboys was acceptable behaviour, however strange the lifestyles of these hormonally charged acrobats was to the western mind, to them it was the way they made their living, they certainly had the necessary qualifications. Most of their earnings were sent home to support their families, many of who lived in the north of mainland Thailand, an area that made Koh Samui look like Eldorado. In this corner of the world money doesn't talk, it swears at the top of it's voice. Whilst the Thai's consider the sale of alcohol and tobacco together with gambling to be unethical, they see nothing wrong in a father selling his daughters to the sex industry or marrying her off in order to receive a dowry from a prospective husband's family when he wants a new house or car. Similarly and bizarrely, the Thai's still consider the act of baring the soles of the feet or touching a persons head in public, to be the height of bad manners, however opening a beer bottle with one's anal orifice seems to be perfectly acceptable, despite these anachronisms the girls still find it acceptable to fondle the farangs, by their standards, enormous breasts, I must admit to having a common interest with this rewarding and enjoyable hobby and have passed many a happy hour honing my skills in pursuance of excellence. Similarly, if a driver is unfortunate enough to be involved in a collision whilst driving his vehicle, or is stopped by the local police whilst 'pissed as a fart', the most serious crime he could possibly commit would be not having sufficient funds to bribe the long arm of the law, the third party and occasionally, the judge.

Apparently the going rate is about ten thousand baht, (£150) when I was enlightened as to the extent of corruption in Thailand, I understood why when I asked Dave how much the jeep insurance was, he just laughed and ordered another beer.

Most evenings I was usually to be found in 'The Office', this was not an offshoot of the renowned

'Langdale Leisure Taverns' conglomerate, but was a sports bar on the main drag in Bangrak, it stood next door too a 'Family Mart'. Whilst sampling a beer one night I wondered if it was possible to purchase a whole family there, in a similar way that a customer could rid themselves of their relatives at the local family butcher or buy a new angle grinder at Machine Mart in the UK. Before I had a chance to complete my manic musings, Trev walked in, apparently not dead and seemingly recovered from his heart attack and imminent appointment with the clouds. Trev, stupidly asked how I was, where upon he was informed in graphic detail that the days greatest pleasure was discussing the quantity, consistency and colour of the mornings toilet deposits and exchanging notes with Dave, 'dropping the kids off at the pool' was so much more interesting in Thailand, if a little more painful, not to put too fine a point on the subject, my arse was leaking like a badly holed Exxon Valdez, and, like it's larger role model it was inevitable that some shoreline or sleepy cove would be the final destination of it's toxic cargo, although I doubt if my contribution to world pollution ever travelled as far as Alaska. Fortunately, my body had slowly returned to a degree of normality, which meant that on occasions I was able to fart with confidence and pass solids once more, unfortunately I was still not certain when these occasions were likely to be. Still, I took comfort from the fact that 'sending a friend to the seaside' had become less of a spectator sport and a whole lot more comfortable of late. Since my arrival in Thailand, I had become concerned that my anal crooning sounded not unlike the collective vocal croaking's of the indigenous tree frog choir after a heavy downpour, having a worryingly loud and protracted refrain. On several occasions, whilst in Thailand, I was rudely reminded of a good friend's prophetic trinity of advice, which he assured me would guide me safely through my twilight years. Rule one, never attempt to put your socks on whilst standing, rule two, never trust a fart and rule three, never waste an erection, even if you are alone at the time. During my stay I didn't wear socks but the remaining advice proved very helpful, for which I am eternally grateful.

One unexpected bonus of my intimate and extended relationship with the porcelain, was that I was able to observe the bathroom's extensive collection of wildlife. Every night I could marvel at the agility of the Geckos and their ability to walk upside down on the ceiling of my personal safari park. I was on first name terms with a three inch Stag beetle who resided behind the bidet, this was not the case with the giant arachnid who laid in wait behind my bedroom door, it's spread was larger than my trembling hand. It grinned vehemently as I entered the room, then raised it's front legs as if preparing to pounce. I resisted the two temptations which immediately crossed my mind, firstly to soil my jeans and secondly, to make the spiders contact with the floor a whole lot more intimate, instead I rescued it with the aid of a large bowl. For such a sizeable beastie it was still pretty rapid in the under the bed and up the wall department, to coin an old Yorkshire Adage, 'it was like shit off a stick'. What I did not realize at the time was the fact that this eight legged Linford was a homing spider, the next evening it had returned complete with it's assortment of tattoos and pet pit-bull, this time it had also invited a few cockroach pals as back up.

During one of my more prolonged confinements in the Armitage Shanks zoo, I was captivated by the most amazing display of teamwork and co-ordination, unfortunately I missed the chance to video the event and thus greatly assist the England cricket coach. The line of ants, each about 5mm long, stretched for five feet up the tiled wall to a small hole. The ants had carried their prize, a dying beetle, which was approximately 3 cm long, across the floor and were busy hoisting the stricken insect upwards, from one ant to the next, in a perfectly timed piece of vertical ballet, it was an ant version of 'pass the parcel', with my bowels providing the accompanying music. I watched, enthralled, as the tiny creatures achieved their task and lowered the beetle, legs still kicking, into the hole. If the relative sizes of the insects were considered their feat became even more amazing, the nearest analogy I could imagine would involve snow white's diminutive house guests hauling a double decker bus up the recently Vaselined exterior of the Empire State building, unlike their cricketing colleagues each ant instinctively knew what it was expected to do and performed it's task faultlessly, they didn't even speak to each other during the ascent.

I walked into the small roadside restaurant, it appeared that the owner had aspirations of being the islands version of a drive through McDonalds, unfortunately his business plan was not as detailed as it could have been. There was only room for one vehicle at a time, this was an obligatory giant 4x4 truck, and was parked slap bang in the centre of the dining area, furthermore the large breezeblock wall prevented the vehicle from moving in any other direction except backwards, the owners culinary innovation didn't appear to be working well. His restaurant had adopted the basic approach with regard to the furnishings, the Axminster carpet perfectly mimicked a well worn concrete floor, principally because that is what it was. The roof was similarly unadorned by down lighters or chandeliers, being constructed of corrugated asbestos sheets and rusting fluorescent tubes. Whilst waiting for the menu, I estimated my chances of surviving the meal, to my mind it appeared to be a three way race. If the carbon monoxide poisoning from the truck or the asbestosis from the roof didn't get me, then the food poisoning from the chicken feet, mixed bowels, fried rags and grubs probably would. Whilst it seemed that the menu had lost a little in translation, (this was later proved not to be the case-it was word perfect), the reality was that my downfall would probably be as a result of a combination of all three. What I hadn't factored into the equation was Thailand's drunken and cerebrally challenged equivalent of Valentino Rossi. His somewhat unorthodox arrival at the restaurant was heralded by a screech of brakes and a large fall out cloud of dust. The remains of his bike slid across the main road and into one side of the dining area, whilst he performed a similar acrobatic routine towards my table, his entrance was, to say the least, less than elegant. To exacerbate the situation, Bambi's stunt double had clearly been shopping at the local cocktail bar and had placed his purchases in the front basket of his now considerably lighter and less aerodynamic moped. As a result of the vehicle's conflagration with the road his newly acquired collection of Molotov cocktails approached me at an unnerving velocity and proximity, fortunately the bottles didn't break and the diners were not party to a large and impromptu BBQ. During my stay, I was reminded on several other occasions that the Thai's struggle with the concept of riding their machines in a vertical manner, although none of the other accidents that I witnessed provided a similar helping of entertainment value and amusement.

Whilst dining, I contemplated Thailand's attitude towards it's principal industry. Sweden had Abba, Britain had red tape and welfare abuse, Thailand had sex. Since the girls were mostly petite and slim, many of them appeared younger than they were, this had the effect of turning the streets into a paedophile's fantasy world, a veritable banquet of temptation. The only exceptions to the rule were the local Samui girls who were instantly recognisable and made Aby's sibling back in Gainsborough look positively svelte like. It appeared incongruous and immoral to see an obese 60 year old man walking through town with an angel, who was one third his age, hanging on to his arm and walking aid, not to mention every word. A walk down any street provided the casual spectator with an identity parade of deviants, every conceivable geek, anorak and pervert had a beautiful young girl with them, amazingly, even some of the Americans had acquired a basic knowledge of the rules of the game. In their home towns most of these men would be firmly ensconced in front of internet screens with a box of tissues and a gimp mask or would be busy rearranging their collection of train numbers and HB pencils. Clearly, this was not the case in Thailand, I never established if these men understood that it was not the contents of their trousers the girls were interested in, more over it was the contents of their wallets.

Slowly, I began to understand what was missing, no matter how hard I searched, I could not find any evidence of the concept of love, apart that is, from the love of money. This was more pronounced than in any other country I have ever visited, in Thailand money was love, the

Thai's obsession with it made my debauched existence appear civilised. This obsession with money was clearly evident each time I saw granddad leave the pharmacy with a sack of Viagra under one arm and a girl young enough to be his grand daughter under the other. In Thailand everybody was searching for something, the bar girls were searching for money and a man to give them a better quality of life, the holidaying couple in the restaurant who gazed silently and vacantly passed each other across the table, were searching for a reason to stay together. After years together they had exhausted conversation, it was probably a fear of loneliness and the loss of half their assets that kept them under the same roof for so long. I was searching for one good reason why I should not follow my heart instead of my brain and grab a small piece of happiness by the balls. Just like the bar girls, love for me had become a vocation which I no longer understood or dared to dream about.

I was about to climb into bed for the night and was busy checking under the quilt for Linford the arachnid's remaining lynch mob, when the text message that would completely and irrevocably change my life, flashed on the screen of my mobile phone. It was my girlfriend informing me that our relationship was over and that she no longer wished to be part of my life, worse still, she had found someone new to replace me. At that moment my body died from the shoulders upwards, within a few days of being on the island I had sorted out my life and determined the way forward, I had mentally penned my final letter to my wife and sorted out my business interests in order that I could start a fresh life on my return. With one text message, I knew my life would never again be the same, I had spent a lifetime looking for her and now she was gone, taking with her my dreams and aspirations, my heart, my soul and my trust. I struggled in vain to understand how, a few weeks earlier, we had shared the same bed and the same dreams, now she had stubbed me out like a midnight cigarette. In my arrogance and naivety, I had assumed that it was only myself who had decisions to make, never once did I contemplate that she might do the same, such was my trust in her. I assumed that the look in her eyes, each time we met, said it all, never once did I think that the windows on her soul were furnished with lace curtains.

For the first time I realised what pain I had subjected my wife to over the years and for the first time I felt guilty and ashamed. I was 6000 miles from the woman I loved, lonely, helpless and broken, I knew I could not stay for the duration, already I was counting the bricks in the walls. In an attempt to save our relationship, I booked the first flight home. The next flight available was almost a week. Seven days, 168 hours, 10080 minutes, 604800 seconds, I counted each one. I realised it doesn't matter where in the world a person may be, however beautiful and idyllic, if you don't have the right partner, you might as well be in Rotherham, for me it is the company not the location which is important.

During the agonisingly long nights I tried to understand how my partner had switched off her feelings for me like a light, more to the point why she felt the need to change the bulb. I knew I had not progressed from my first days at secondary school, I had been usurped by a younger man with a car, assets, a future, a house and no baggage, I was still metaphorically using the school bus and had acquired a very heavy satchel. More importantly, my rival was a golfer, that I most certainly could not compete with, like my distrust of the clergy, I viewed golfers with a sense of unease. I found it difficult to' understand the wardrobe reasoning of grown men who wore bright pink trousers, one glove and spiked shoes, when they had no intention of running anywhere, I knew I should never have trusted a man whose fashion role model was Rupert Bear, now I wished that my rival had continued to use a tee to rest his balls on instead of the love of my life's velvet tardis, from this day onwards she would be forever known as the nineteenth hole, and remains the only women I know whose legs have different postcodes.

Throughout my life I had firmly believed that money could not buy happiness, now I reasoned a little more would at least allow me to be miserable in a greater degree of comfort. My Ying and Yang had had an almighty argument and disappeared westwards in a colossal supernova, or as the doctor later explained in simple medical terms I'd gone mad and had a certificate to prove it. Overnight, my life had become empty and my brain numb with a pain, the likes of which, I had never experienced before, I didn't need the plane to get me home, I simply cried my way back to Manchester

SUICIDE IS PAINLESS (MY ARSE)

I guess that I always knew that at some point in my weird little world, it was going to go 'tit's up'. I had after all read the beginners guide to adultery and noted that the eventual outcome was always predictable. With this certainty firmly lodged in my one remaining functioning brain cell, I formulated an emergency action plan, one that was only to be used in the direst emergency, and most certainly not in a flippant way like a get out of jail card in the world's most boring and futile game. Without a doubt this was a last ditch, one use only, default position not to be initiated in any situation other than one of the most shittiest of shit, insurmountable, no way out scenarios. I determined that I would have to kill myself, there was nothing else for it. It was the only logical route to take, the only prudent course of action which would be best for all concerned.

With the benefit of hindsight, I am now able to see the flaws in this flash of inspiration, namely that my master plan was ill thought out and shit, with a capital S. To say that my plan was something less than perfect would be somewhat short of the mark, in a similar way that asserting that Dawn French was the doyen of the British hang gliding team would doubtless cause considerable hilarity and embarrassment at the bar of the local aeronautical club. In short it was doomed to failure from the start. Firstly, when considering my options and determining which course of action would be the most beneficial for all concerned, I hadn't really done the maths, or rather, I had but in truth my results would have been more accurate if I had used a calculator, preferably one with a fully charged battery and functioning logic circuits. I had neither! For a start my master plan would most certainly not be beneficial for me, in fact I reasoned, with a certain degree of accuracy and authority, it would almost certainly have the opposite effect on my well being. Even in my darkest hour I was able to comprehend that me being fatally dead was not going to help me at all. True it may be of benefit to Lady Langdale and son, who would, no doubt, have being better off without me, moreover the 19th hole was no doubt too busy getting pissed, high and laid (not necessarily in that order) to even notice my untimely demise, in any eventuality, she had already made it abundantly clear that she didn't give a 'flying fuck' about my welfare.

Still, undeterred, I soldiered on with instruction one from the 'Do it yourself death manual for boys' and thrust myself headlong into my ill conceived plan, namely how to bring about my unscheduled end. It was at this time that I remembered my formative years when I had found myself in a similar situation. I was seventeen spotty years old, and my long term girl friend of some two months-Monday to Friday, i.e., school days inclusive, unceremoniously ditched me for another pupil of life's rocky road. She had discovered that my alleged 'love pad' in rural Yorkshire was my mum and dad's three bed semi-in Rotherham and my super-cool four wheeled pulling limousine was actually a shagged out MK II Vauxhall Viva with a worrying lack of brakes and an inherent smell of piss whenever the rain permeated it's rotten colander like body-work, which in truth was about as scabby as a leper's arse with a serious haemorrhoid problem, in the Peoples Republic of South Yorkshire, this precipitation was generally to be found when there was a 'Y' in the day. Looking back, it would probably be more accurate to deduce that my premature dumping on the rubbish heap of love, was not so much due to my lack of assets and wealth, nor indeed the crap car that I owned, but was more likely to have been the result of my burgeoning desire for Swarfega and cable ties in the vicinity of the den of depravity that was previously referred to as my bedroom. I recollect that we had often argued about our little 'struggle snuggles', as I liked to call them, I recall that my assertion that there was no such thing as rape and that a girl should merely consider the whole operation to be surprise sex, did nothing to placate her or, improve the atmosphere. On reflection our relationship was doomed from its inception for no other reason than I was turning into a predatory sexual deviant of the first magnitude,

146

perhaps that was the reason why the lesbian bitch didn't return my Camel and Yes albums and burned my kaftan.

At the time, my juvenile solution to the suicide problem was, on reflection possibly a little over simplified. I determined to wank myself to death, simple as it was, this severe course of action proved to be less than expedient and somewhat badly thought out, not to mention painful. After two weeks of diligent onanism, all I had to show for my exhaustive efforts were painful calluses on both hands, RSI to my now arthritic elbows and a prick that looked like a pound of liver. (well, a good couple of ounces at least) I also suspected that my strategy was having a detrimental effect on my failing eyesight. My mother, meanwhile, was struggling to comprehend the apparent dearth of toilet roll in the family bathroom, at one time, she even blamed the unexplained shortage on the neighbour whose IBS was well documented and discussed around the dinner table, unsurprisingly the lady in question then refused to speak to her for some considerable time. For sure, in our street, mother was better known for her knitting abilities than her tact and diplomacy, if she had by some strange twist of fate, landed a job at the Samaritans, within a very short time the local suicide figures would have risen faster than Tiger Wood's prick in a brothel. Similarly she struggled to conceive what had become of the catering size pack of man size tissues, which she had recently bought from the local cash and carry, my father merely pondered as to why the pages of his Daily Mirror were often to be found solidly cemented together, usually in the vicinity of page three, or were partially or wholly missing, secretly I guess he always knew I was a wanker and knew exactly who the culprit was, although he did initially blame the poor quality of cheap Chinese newsprint. With the benefit of hindsight I can now see that Dad was simply being polite.

In truth, my first pathetic attempt at self inflicted death by wanking was always going to be an unqualified failure, for sure, I would have probably achieved better results had I tried to concuss myself with a budgie's tail feather. For a start I had been a leading exponent of the art since my early teenage years and was thus immune to its effects. I was a world class wanker, it soon became apparent that a couple more tugs a day wouldn't hurt my 'match fit body'. My New Years resolutions that particular year, were to stop smoking and wanking. This was imperative in the interests of my health, since I had a twenty a day habit and, worse still, I smoked to excess.

With the passing of the years and the benefit of a rudimentary education it was clear that a rerun of plan A would be something of a non-starter, my current predicament would require a far more complicated, thoroughly thought out, logical strategy to extricate me from the mire in which I now found myself.

So it was, that in common with most would be suicide candidates of a physically lazy disposition, I deduced that the B in plan B stood for binge, for sure the quickest, most efficient route to Death City was to drink myself there, no need for a stage coach just copious amounts of alcohol. Unfortunately, unlike my earlier attempts at world wanking domination, when it came to drinking, I soon discovered a problem, namely that I wasn't very good at it. It had often been a source of amusement to me as to why young men and latterly ladies, I use the term in the loosest possible way, as indeed I would likewise catalogue Susan Boyle, feel the urge to fight the world and abuse any unfortunate bystander after imbibing a couple of pints of piss weak British lager (probably the shittiest lager in the world). Throughout my life, whenever I found myself in an alcohol fuelled mess, my ambitions were not for world domination, rather, I preferred to fall asleep and dribble from various orifices in varying degrees, the last notion on my mind was anything in the least bit strenuous, such as world domination, that could most certainly wait for another day when my head wasn't banging and my legs and bowels were behaving themselves and answering to authority. Throughout history, the archive films have seldom depicted Adolf Hitler, standing in front of the Reichstag, with a large piss stain on his trousers or a six inch snot candle festooning his face and nasal apertures, whilst addressing a rally of the Hitler youth, world domination and alcohol just do not work!

I realised that my newly formulated scheme for self annihilation would require a certain amount of diligence and determination on my part and would not come to fruition overnight. With this in mind I set about consuming more than my fair share of alcohol, like an apprentice Oliver Reed. Getting hold of the stuff was easy since I owned a pub and a brewery and thus did not have to resort to Domestos or Brasso, it couldn't be simpler, 24 hour death juice was available on tap any hour of the day. Since my return from Thailand my brain, like my bowels had been unable to function at anything like its full potential, the former being as a result of being ditched by Miss Troon the latter being as a direct result of imbibing over ambitious quantities of red wine and Guinness, my alimentary canal was rapidly turning into a Chernobyl like meltdown, with all too often, similar explosive consequences, my reactor had gone critical and the resultant fallout would take an inordinate amount of cleaning up. My mind and body had decided to emulate a nineteen sixties Lambretta scooter by constantly breaking down, unfortunately I wasn't doing as many miles to the gallon, but our smoking habits were similar.

One side effect of plan B, that was similar to my earlier attempt at self death, was that both strategies resulted in a serious shortage of

Andrex two ply. My constitution was further aggravated by the fact that, on most days, I either forgot or simply could not be bothered to eat, food had become somewhat extraneous, an afterthought that interfered with my drinking. As any engineer of hydraulics will relate it is not prudent to put solids in a hydraulic system, it buggers it up! It was readily apparent to anyone who knew me that I was in the throes of a very severe and uncontrolled mental breakdown. Two years of attempting to make decisions about my life, which, with the benefit of hindsight, I now realise, I was totally unqualified to make, but which I had nevertheless tried in a most incompetent and ineffectual way to achieve, had taken its toll. In an act of revenge my mind had 'called time' on logic and the workers had downed tools and walked out on strike. I found it impossible to carry out simple tasks which previously were second nature. The only tasks I could now perform with a certain degree of ability and dexterity were crying inconsolably and muttering uncontrollably, I was also reasonable adept at feeling sorry for myself. Never in my life, thus far, had I believed that it was possible for one person to feel so much sadness and loneliness, it seemed that nothing had any relevance anymore, I felt I couldn't go back and I didn't relish the thought of going forward. Life had lost any relevance or reason, dreams and aspirations, much like plasma widescreen TVs and broadband, became the idylls that normal happy individuals had. It was as if someone had thrown a switch and my mind, starved of life's electricity and drive, had been irrevocably darkened, my life spark had dimmed, flickered and farted itself off into the ether on a one way ticket to oblivion, along with it went all the things that made me, me. Sure I was still physically healthy, going through life's mundane routines, even if I did have a habit of shitting myself at inopportune times, but my soul, my Psyche, my me, had died. All the feelings, thoughts anachronisms and nuances that had built my personality over 40 odd years, from my early nappy filling days had vanished, almost overnight, quicker than a newly shod set of alloys in a Gainsborough car park. I was left well and truly resting on a couple of bricks in a shit strewn hole. In short I never realised what a dark, lonely place depression was, but for sure, now I was going to get plenty of practice in the dark art.

The one light in this chasm of darkness was Lady Langdale's understanding, tolerance and love, to this day, in keeping with most of my friends and family, I cannot comprehend how someone who had been shat upon (is that the correct past participle of shit?) from such a great height, could still find it in her heart and soul to care for and forgive the perpetrator. She had always been competent at jigsaws but this metaphorical one was going to test even her extraordinary abilities. In truth Stevie Wonder and Ray Charles would probably have been given similar odds on the chances of success at the local bookies, undeterred, she set about trying to wrestle my shattered mind from out of the darkness, kick start the generator and reignite my spark, or, as she so eloquently put it in nursing terms, kick me up the arse and tell me to stop feeling sorry for myself.

Judgement Day

What I had no way of knowing during my futile efforts at self destruction, was the fact that it was all a waste of time. Certainly I knew that one day the big man in the sky would precipitate my demise, what I was blissfully unaware of, and I blame him 100% for not having the common decency to keep me 'in the loop,' was that, in his unquestioned omnipotence and unbounded knowledge, he had decided to bring my demise date forward somewhat, in fact, he had already picked me for the following Saturday's 5-a-side friendly against Hell United. God knows why, but during our one and only encounter he wasn't telling. Instead, he just sat there, on his throne, on cloud number 10, which is situated next door and a little upmarket from Happy Larry and his lesser mortal chums on Cloud 9. He was sporting an inane grin, holding a four pack of special brew in one hand and a hand rolled fag in the other. Apparently most of his time is now spent perusing the myriad banks of CCTV screens in his front office in order to keep tabs on his vestal virgins, all the dead dogs at the end of the drive named Rex and trying to differentiate which dead Smith is which, unfortunately the influx of Eastern Europeans, with their respective surnames, is causing a real headache up in heaven, to the point where he has had to fork out £100 an hour for interpreters. Unsurprisingly, since the interventions of Lady Ashton and her parasitic side kicks in Brussels, he is now inundated with Health and Safety regulations and risk assessments, as a result of current employment laws all the angels are now male, (it saved on the cost of lady angel toilets) the only good thing to arise from the new legislation is the fact that the over officious fire officer is now on permanent call out downstairs. When death gets too much for God and boredom sets in, apparently he relaxes by precipitating as much sadness and destruction, to us mere mortals, as his Godly powers allow, since he makes the rules he pretty much seems to have 'free range' in the misery and destruction department. A touch of pestilence, famine or Bubonic plague evidently lifts his spirits, indeed, he has even being known to detonate the odd Icelandic Volcano just to piss off Mr O'Leary and his Ryan Air empire, apparently God never forgave one of his pilots for buzzing a BBQ in his back garden a couple of years ago. In truth, God really is a ruthless, evil bastard!

At the side of God's throne sits a crate of lager and an enormous pile of writs and solicitors letters, on the back wall a large aerosol encrusted banner proclaims Billy Connelly to be a cunt, when I enquired as to what the meaning of this was, he explained that until the release of BC's film nobody had even considered the simple expedient of suing him when their insurance company would not pay out for his acts. In common with most litigation cases he is now inundated with the damned things, to the point that his latest risk assessment stated that the mounting piles of paper work posed a serious fire threat to all the dead people's health, and was an accident waiting to happen.

What most members of the public, down here on earth, are totally unaware of is that, since the recession, the cut backs have really begun to bite in the land of eternity and damnation. Things have got so bad that his counterpart down under was made redundant and now resides in a caravan park in Lowestoft and makes ends meet with a part time position at UKIP and occasionally moonlights by performing mass in the Catholic church on Sundays. It is double time and he needs the money, apparently the 'minge' benefits' are pretty good too.

God, meanwhile, job shares and splits his time booking in new arrivals at the pearly gates, or rather where they used to be before the Gippos had them away for scrap, and overseeing the stoking of the furnaces and rotas for eternal damnation in Hell. Understandably fatigue and boredom take their toll. Hence on June 19th 2007 after a busy day at the Heaven reception desk, I was to become the source of God's amusement, there was obviously nothing of any interest on Sky TV, the cherubs were all on a staff training day, as per new Brussels requirements, and the two angels on duty that day, who just happened to be gay, had secured union rights to paternity leave in order to look after their newly acquired surrogate Somalian child. Thus, God was obviously bored as fuck and alone with all the facilities of the universe at his disposal.

Peculiarly, since it was probably the most important and eventful day of my life thus far, I have few recollections of the evenings events, which as a result of God's ennui, unfolded before me. Actually, to be more precise, they unfolded in front of my much prized Harley Davidson motorcycle. The big man played the double bastard joker card and lulled me into a false sense of security by providing a very pleasant summers evening, really I should have known better and realised that something was amiss, in my experience sunshine in June, in Britain, is always to be treated with the utmost suspicion and is usually the harbinger of doom. His dastardly plan worked a treat and like a prize twat I shunned my usual protective leathers for a fleece and jeans, I reasoned that since I was only travelling the few miles home on a route which I routinely accomplished, on a daily basis without hither to any previous consequences or incident, everything would be fine. The consequences of this particular balmy evening were, in a split second, to irrevocably change my life forever. To this day, I have no comprehension of what really happened, although the more cynical and gossip prone members of the pubs clergy and congregation assumed, quite wrongly, that I had instigated plan C of the 'which guide to self suicide'. The 'C' in question standing for Crash and a very large, serious and painful one at that. My colleagues of the local biking fraternity had always ridiculed Willy G's fifty year old technology as been somewhat outdated and agricultural. Usually they referred to my much loved Milwaukee steel chariot as being a Hardley-moving son tractor, unfortunately my chosen mode of transport decided to revert to type and attempted to plough a long, deep furrow in a local farmers field. To make matters worse it completed its newly choreographed party piece together with a triple somersault and a half pike whilst I was still firmly ensconced in the saddle, and more worryingly still hanging on to the handlebars, as though my life depended on them. Sadly, at that moment in time it almost certainly did. The local Friesian community, knowing nothing of God's sick and evil sense of humour, apart that is that they suspected him of instigating several outbreaks of foot and mouth, BSE and udder rash, were to say the least bemused and somewhat startled at the sight of a middle aged incompetent and incontinent biker tumbling through their midst at tea time, no doubt they considered my unscheduled intrusion at the very least, a little rude not to mention inconsiderate and somewhat un-neighbourly.

Suddenly my mid-life crisis was about to metamorphose into an end of life version of the same, with the added ingredients of extra pain and suffering on my part. Thankfully, I was totally unaware of the evenings proceedings, lying as I was totally incapacitated and face down in piles of cold rancid cow shit, blood and pools of extreme agony.

The last fleeting recollection of my previous life involved me overtaking a large motor home. Fortunately, for me, the driver had observed my impromptu acrobatic display and was now transfixed in awe and utter amazement at the Tom and Jerry like silhouette in the perimeter Hawthorne of my eventual resting place, which had suddenly appeared as a consequence of the combined weight and inertia of myself and the bike bursting through it at terminal, (well very nearly) velocity. The more adventurous and forward thinking cows ensconced there in, were already well advanced with their plans for their imminent escape and ensuing night on the town, when Mr Happy the local farmer rolled up to curtail their exodus and cut short any vacation plans by recourse to some fence posts and hastily procured timber.

Lady Langdale, who by now had become worried by my late return, chose the moment that the ambulance arrived on scene to call me on my mobile phone. Undoubtedly, it was not the most pleasant experience of her life to be informed by the paramedic that her significant other half was about to be scraped up off the ground, put in a bucket and whisked off to the local ITU, operating theatre or morgue, dependant on various variables, the main one being whether or not I continued to breath. No doubt her displeasure was further compounded by the paramedics comment that I was covered from head to toe in cow shit and that she really should take more care of my under pants, since it was difficult to tell where the me ended and the cow started, shameful.

Due to their proximity, my wife and son were soon on scene and joined the assembled throng which by now was beginning to resemble a cross between a last rites mass, of an alfresco variety, and a perverse cow pat orientated version of 'Twister', with the ever swelling congregation carefully stepping through the faecal minefield on tiptoes to gaze at the soon to be deceased corpse.

At this point God was winning 2-0 on aggregate, but just to ensure his total emphatic victory he now employed his Coup De Grace, he instantaneously opened every valve and sluice at his disposal at the stratospheric waterworks, thus creating a wall of ice cold water, a veritable curtain of liquid stair rods, as the heavens opened he then proceeded to add a pinch of fork lightning and a scintilla of thunder, just to show off. What a total and complete twat, not only was I nearly deceased but I was now soaked to the skin as well, just when I considered my life really could not get much worse, as always, this was proven not to be the case. Dodging reasonably solid, thixotropic cow shit is one thing, avoiding cold cow shit soup is another far more complicated concept. My rout and very nearly my life, now completed, I could picture a smug looking God, resplendent in his newly ironed robes, strolling down to his local to gloat. I wager he couldn't wait to relate to his mates the days events and the pain and upset he had instigated 'Ere Pete, what a fucking hoot I've had today, you remember that arrogant twat from the pub in Gainsborough, that's him, the one trying to juggle with his wife and girlfriend, always following his cock around, well I stopped him in his tracks, he won't be doing that anymore, he's left it on the handlebars of a Harley Davidson in a field near Bawtry. Best fun I've had for ages, yes Pete even better than fingering that new Thai angel with the cute arse and pert wings'.

My all too intimate, encounters with the grass and micro fauna of the verdant pasture was in short not an experience I would wish to repeat anytime soon, neither, according to the account which my son gave of his journey as he accompanied me in the ambulance to hospital, was my deliverance to Doncaster Royal Infirmary courtesy of the NHS meat delivery agency. I can only assume that the admissions unit was somewhat short staffed and that Jensen Button coincidentally had taken an annual leave day from racing to help out. Apparently, if the vehicle had been fitted with a pair of wings it would have flown to its destination at the local

ITU, such was its velocity, resplendent with sirens and flashing strobe lights. Fortunately, I remained totally unaware off the jaunt, being as I was, smacked off my tits on copious amounts of morphine. Neither did I have any sight of the rapidly passing landscape since I was firmly attached to an aptly named body board and my shattered spine was equally firmly secured with various braces and restraints, which would undoubtedly have made Harry Houdini or a bondage freak and his pet gimp feel at home. On reflection I would dearly have liked to have seen more of the journey and particularly the Doncaster bus lane, since on previous visits, I had only being able to observe it at the giddy speed attainable by a one legged elderly and fatigued leprous snail with breathing problems and a particularly troublesome in growing toenail, such was the traffic congestion caused by the endless queues of tax paying, car driving, individuals who had endeavoured to complete the daily commute to work, what fools. Typical of my luck, the first time I was allowed as a mere tax- paying individual minion to travel on this traffic free elite highway, without receiving a ticket from the over zealous plod, I was totally incapable of enjoying the trip or savouring it's pleasures. On many occasions, usually whilst stuck in traffic, in the adjacent lane, I had pondered the logic of this superhighway, built no doubt, at great expense to the local tax and rate payers and to the detriment and frustration of local drivers.   Although the planners of this seemingly logical idea had widened the road and provided Park and Ride stations to facilitate the desired, swift and uncongested passage of the passenger less buses into the centre of Doncaster, for some peculiar unknown reason, which to this day remains a secret, they had not considered repeating the operation for the outward journey. Since the only road leading out of town, which runs parallel to the inbound journey, only has one lane and is always nose to tail with the very traffic which the system was presumably designed to avoid, the system appears, to my simple mind, to be very much a one way, inward bound, no exit, no u-turn, type of affair which only seems to succeed in winding up motorists like myself, who paid for the half baked idea in the first place, never mind the fact that in anyone's book, it is a pretty obvious fucking design flaw. I can only conclude that somewhere in the centre of town, there is either a large black hole, which swallows commuters on a daily basis, or that there is a field full of the poor souls, standing around in a bewildered and abandoned state, wondering how on earth they will ever get home or be repatriated with their vehicles in the Park and Ride, some five miles away, no wonder the buses are empty, there are obviously no commuters left. Little wonder then that the authorities made the car parks so vast, presumably inside a week they were destined to become full to overflowing, since none of their owners were ever able to return, instead, they were cursed until eternity to wander in a kind of bureaucratic twilight zone, laptops and Blackberries in hand. Come the revolution brothers, the architects of this inane scheme, together with their council accomplices, will undoubtedly be the first to be lined up against the wall, second only to the one eyed Scottish bastard and his Royal Toniness of the house of Orange who between them managed quite successfully to financially and morally bankrupt the nation, whilst surprisingly, doing quite alright thank you very bloody nicely for themselves.

Recently, I have learned that in some towns such as Doncaster, motorists whilst whiling their traffic queuing hours away in a stationary manner, are now being prosecuted for the heinous crime of discarding cigarette butts out of the windows of their vehicles, some drivers are even picking up fines and points on their licences for turning to look at the leggy young lady sporting a pussy pelmet and tight top on a summers day, and who are thus deemed, by the overzealous and officious plod, to be driving without due care and attention. This is the result of the wonder of modern science that is CCTV, whilst I do not for one moment condone wilful littering, and would indeed gladly shoot on sight anybody found in possession of a Macdonald's bag for exactly that reason, I am somewhat bemused and confused that the same authorities, and their servants, find it beyond their capabilities to investigate much more serious lawbreaking incidents such as burglaries, assaults and thefts or to convict the local low life scrap thieves every time that they help themselves to the lead which used to adorn my local church roof, even when the same authorities are provided with CCTV footage, names and addresses of culprits or indeed even when the protagonists are caught red handed , after risking my own neck in a protracted struggle. Still at least I am not bitter, I simply find it incredible and totally unsatisfactory, as a tax payer and law abiding citizen, that the CPS fails to throw the full force of the law, for what it's worth, since it has about as much weight as a Biafran supermodel with an eating disorder, pancreatitis and mild liver failure, at the real criminals, instead the lefty tree hugging liberal minded lentil eaters prefer to give the bastards an asbo and a cuddle and blame it all on society and the fact that their mothers failed to breastfeed the poor little mites well into their teenage years. Meanwhile we are told that there is insufficient evidence to obtain a conviction, probably because the court case would cost too much and damage the defendants minds and be detrimental to their leisure time, and in any event, doubtless the local prison/hotel will be full. If I was of a cynical disposition, I would suggest that the former would provide our representatives with an easy eighty quid towards their Christmas party fund, whilst the latter would undoubtedly cost the tax payer dearly. Personally, if I had my way, I would nail the offenders bollocks to the gate post of the church, just a little too high up for their owners to be truly comfortable. When the offending articles shrivelled up and rotted off, I would throw their emasculated owners in prison, four to a cell, make them shit in a communal bucket, preferably with a broken handle, and make them eat their own snot until such time as they determined never to reoffend. In order to ensure their rehabilitation, I would piss on their PS3's and plasma TV's, remove the mattresses from their beds and superglue the pages of their wank mags together. What a bizarre and twisted society we now inhabit, where it is acceptable to remove eight hundred year old roofing materials from a national treasure without retribution or penalty, but woe betide the poor unfortunate who inadvertently discards a scrap of rubbish and whose bank account as a result is depleted to the tune of eighty quid, the whole scenario almost makes dear old uncle Adolf look quite benevolent and well worth voting for at the next election.

HOSPITALS AND HOTELS

So it was, as in all the best bible stories, it came to pass that the tower of mediocrity of the biking world, i.e. me, resplendent with standard issue broken heart, broken bones and soiled jeans was dutifully delivered via Doncaster Royal Infirmary sorting office to Sheffield's Northern General Hospital, more precisely the spinal injuries unit, in order that the orthopaedic consultants had something to practice on and giggle at/talk about in the pub on a Friday night, and the nursing staff had something to humiliate and ridicule as best their powers and implements would allow. The unit on which I had been unceremoniously dumped reminded me of an earlier episode in my corrupt and depraved life. More particularly it was the communal sleeping arrangements which jogged my dormant memory. I recall being around the tender age of seventeen, just prior to my now legendary world endurance wanking efforts, on this occasion I, along with a dozen or so other A level geography students, had been deposited in an unsuspecting hotel in Llandudno, North Wales for the annual field trip. The more advanced students of the drinking and copulating class had amalgamated with similar minded forces from another equally delinquent and depraved institution, to share information and bodily fluids. I recall the culmination of this meeting of minds was an impromptu (ménage a neuf) or, as it has now become known in certain parts of North Wales by various hotel owners and police officers, a 'cluster fuck'. For sure, there was a greater amount of meat on display than the butchery counter of the local Tesco Extra. In short, it was an uncontrolled outburst of passion, fumbling and in some cases learning, an unbridled cornucopia of copulation which previously I had only witnessed in nature documentaries involving crabs, certain species of amphibians and over sexed jelly fish. The melee was a prehistoric throwback to some depraved age where the hole was most definitely the goal, like the machinations of the embryonic Ernie, any number, any order, any position with every participant a winner. Caligula would most certainly have felt very much at home. It could only have been the fact that the Marquis De Said rarely holidayed in that particular are of North Wales in April that precluded his attendance at the shindig, that or the fact that he had been dead for some considerable time. Nevertheless it was a memorable evening's filth and debauchery for all concerned which left a deeply embedded memory on my developing adolescent grey matter. In truth, it was a pity that the Marquis was not in attendance, since I am pretty certain that he would not have 'legged it' tout suite, down the rear fire escape when the hotel's landlady came rapping on the bedroom door, during the mid-session interval, to announce the imminent arrival of the local constabulary. For sure, judging by the ferocity of her knock, she wasn't there to bring cake and refreshments to the proceedings. Meanwhile, I, in conjunction with my newly discovered fuck buddies, were similarly about to announce our own arrivals in a somewhat messier, noisier and far more enjoyable manner. It was only the sight of my accomplice, Perry (ex woodwork class/plane incident) attempting to hurriedly replace his shirt and shoes whilst trying to negotiate the slippery metal fire escape with his jeans around his ankles and a condom hanging from this now limp appendage, which brought the evenings entertainment to a sad and somewhat abrupt end. The evenings rain ensured that the reluctant acrobat bounced from arse cheek to arse cheek in a downward manner, his less than agile efforts were witnessed by most of the hotels residents who had rushed to their windows to discover the source of the noise and wonder at the fun and humiliation to be had at his expense. In short, it was a pathetic and somewhat unsuccessful attempt to make good his quiet and dignified exit, he eventually reached the bottom of the stairs only to suffer the embarrassment of having to reclimb the whole stair case when he discovered that this socks, watch and wallet hadn't bothered to make the initial journey and were still lying in a pile in the middle of the floor, accompanied by another eight pairs of the same and a plethora of condom packets.

The mountain of contraceptives came about as a result of the one useful thing I can ever recall, Perry accomplishing, spurred on by a few pints of lager, he duly dropkicked the vending machine in the adjoining hotel's conveniences in a truly incongruent display of athleticism, which promptly saw the machines contents deposited on the floor, what a result, free fucks all week, yippee! (This was obviously in the days before teenage girls were aware of the going rate for the job) as a result we had more rubber available than the pit land at Silverstone on race day, we tried all the usual obvious ways to deplete our stocks, but when putting them over our heads and blowing them up in an attempt to emulate extra terrestrials didn't work we had to invent a new use. We duly filled them with water and threw them out of the hotel windows at unsuspecting pedestrians, the entertainment went well until the unsuspecting passer by happened to be our geography master. Although he was a bigger sex pest than the rest of the class combined, he clearly did not appreciate being assaulted by copious amounts of latex and cold water. The mood was lightened somewhat when the launcher of the offending missiles was questioned by his colleagues as to the accuracy of his aims, since we were bravely hiding behind the curtains and could not therefore see the action. 'It missed his shoulder by six inches' he proclaimed, the disappointment was tangible as it filled the room with an aura of despair, our spirits, however, were immediately lifted when he announced 'it hit him smack on the fucking head' the jubilation resounded with 'high fives' all round.

The juvenile game, fun as it was, was nothing compared to the entertainment to be enjoyed when confronted by the appearance of a fellow class mate, a middleclass, teenage vision of Catholic naivety who had heard about Perry's right footed accuracy with the vending machine and decided that now was the time to revolt against her assigned religion and parents rules of conduct, to be more precise she was wholly intent on getting herself some serious cock action. To be even more precise, she was intent on getting young Mr Copaloadathis's cock into action. The victim was a half Greek student whose metaphoric balalaika she had, had her eyes on for the entre trip. Her enthusiasm was barely dampened after seeing the effects on his manhood which had been brought about by his enforced wading in Welsh mountain tarns of liquid mercury at − 273 degrees. Although our geography teacher assured us that this physical torture was both essential and instructive for our education and would further our understanding of the subject, we probably quite rightly, assumed that he was just being a sadistic and vindictive bastard with a dislike of being hit in the face with condoms full of cold water, and teenage A level students with more hope of getting a shag than he had, since he did not subject himself to the same extreme paddling activities, his extremities were not exposed to the elements which, no doubt in his warped mind , gave him a definite size advantage in the 'find yourself a willing school girl stakes'.

The young lady in question, who will remain nameless in order to protect her and any subsequent offspring's reputation, was duly given a three pack and sent on her merry voyage of discovery. During breakfast, the next morning, the conversation turned to condom bomb throwing, although obviously not loud enough for the staff to overhear. This wasn't that difficult since most of them had been dispatched by the extremely irate owner of the hotel, with implicit instructions to clean up the fall out from our target range, i.e. the frontage of the hotel and pavement, in an attempt to minimize the effect on the local canine and feline population who had reportedly been choking on the prophylactics, this phenomenon was apparently worsened by the contraceptive devices in question being of the flavoured variety. Rumour has it that the local Labradors loved the chocolate variety best of all. The conversation was going well until a physics student let slip that, in his humble opinion, the condom bombs would be far more effective and accurate if the condoms used had been stronger and not full of holes, he further asserted that the problem was that they split too easily. The discussion was brought to a sudden and abrupt conclusion by the sound of a young, now not so naïve, catholic girl at the back of the room fainting face first into her porridge, before collapsing in a jibbering heap on the floor.

Just in case any would be travellers or fellow deviants, on reading these few pages, have been motivated and intrigued by the pleasures of mind and body to be had from the geology, topography and demography of North Wales in winter and are considering a similar jaunt to the depths of depravity. Unfortunately, I must report that, according to rumour, the hotel in question sadly no longer accepts A level students. I suspect that it was not purely the threats from the police and local magistrates to rescind their licences which initiated this decision, but also the discovery, after our departure, that the door locks no longer worked since there were no longer any doors and that most of the beds now resembled futons, being like their recent occupants totally legless and extremely soiled, furthermore the en-suite from room two was now mostly in room four and the ceramic wash basin in the adjoining room had mysteriously developed a hole through its middle which to the trained eye closely resembled the shape of a half bottle of Martell Cognac. I sincerely hope that the landlady was not interned for too long and that eventually she made a full recovery in order that she could oversee the refurbishment of her pride and joy.

Industrial quality suspended ceiling tiles, such as those found on hospital wards, are incredibly intricate and interesting objects when studied upfront and personal, to the casual observer they may appear to be dull and mundane but closer examination, and a trained eye, reveals them to be truly amazing and artistic articles, especially when there is fuck all else to look at and you are bored shitless for weeks on end, being as I was, unable to move just about every part of my bruised and battered body, apart from my eyeballs. Perhaps I found them intriguing because I had nothing better to do or perhaps my interest was solely due to the fact that I had downed sufficient drugs to keep a medium sized young offenders institution going for several months, not to put too fine a point on the matter, I was smacked off my face on everything from Paracetamol to morphine, drugs to make me shit, drugs to stop me shitting, drugs to make me sleep, drugs to prevent my blood clotting, drugs to prevent gastric ulcers brought on by the other drugs, ect. I was so full of drugs, I swear that the straps on the bed were provided to prevent me from floating away into the ether of never-never land. The thoughtful staff had even provided me with a magic piece of equipment called a 'driver syringe', a powered pump device which delivered a measured amount of morphine on demand by simply pushing a button. Looking back the term driver syringe seems something of a misnomer, the health and safety brigade and insurance risk assessors would shit themselves en-masse if patients were discovered driving vehicles with a self priming, class A injection device strapped to their arm. Besides, why take the car, when with a push of a button it was possible to fly. No wonder then that my memories of my hospital holiday are at best sketchy and quite possibly, wholly inaccurate. The one memory I do recall with a great degree of accuracy was the relentless, debilitating pain. The seemingly innocuous and normal action of a person breathing over my hyper sensitive skin would result in severe pain which felt as though I was been used as a pin cushion undergoing an assault by hundreds of blunt needles which had recently been removed from a furnace. Morphine is a wonderful drug but it has its limits, it is for example next to useless when the patients mother decides to deposit her fully laden, larger than average handbag on his abdomen at visiting time, I know this from personal experience, silly woman!

My injuries were such that I could barely move any part of my body, except for from the knees down, since these were also knackered from years of long distance running, the prognosis did not look good. I could not even pick my nose or scratch my arse, indeed my wife's first duties at visiting time were usually to rearrange my nose scabs and scratch my offending body parts. In order to alleviate my pain and reduce the risk of bed sores developing, as is usual with prolonged confinement to bed, the hospital had provided an air mattress, an amazing piece of modern computer controlled equipment which pumped compressed air into pockets on its surface in order that my body could be gently massaged and the points of skin contact constantly changed. This was cutting edge technology, which no doubt would have worked well and relieved my pain considerably, if the technician had taken the time to explain to the retarded member of staff charged with my well being, that, in order for it to function, in anything like an efficient and optimum way, it required the 13AMP plug to be inserted into a magic socket on the wall and duly switched on. Still, it only took the staff three days to discover their error, by which time I had won the Sheffield heat of the 2007 Mr Bed Sore competition, newcomer category. With hindsight, it would have been a little discourteous to disturb the staff's tea, biscuits, cake and chocolate breaks and the inevitable gossip as to who was shagging who and how they were looking forward to the evenings rogering, personally, I just hoped they could wait until the shift was over before the proceedings commenced.

The electronically operated bed was another great piece of equipment, which at the touch of a keypad could raise and lower various sections to make the patient more comfortable. Unfortunately, the required keypad was always placed tantalisingly close, but just far enough away as to be impossible to reach, in truth the staff might as well have placed it in a cave on Mars. Every two hours a team of six would turn and manhandle my delicate body, I soon learned to dread this operation, but my resistance was futile, my body had started to imitate the inertia of a lazy quadriplegic and was pretty much fixed to the spot, an incredibly uncomfortable spot at that. The same staff had perfected a similar trick with food and tea as they had with the bed controller, for devilment they would place the offerings on the table over the bed, totally unattainable to my immobile limbs, I figured that after several days they would notice that I had had no sustenance, but they never did. It was not hard to imagine these same staff pulling the legs off spiders or blunting hypodermic needles with an angle grinder during their tea breaks, fortunately Lady Langdale would inevitably bring a Red Cross parcel at visiting time in order too alleviate my suffering. All the same, for months I craved a warm cup of tea, rather than the cold excuse for the same which would eventually be served from a babies anti spill cup, usually on the following day.

Another constant source of bemusement, to my morphine soaked brain, were the numbers of relatives and visitors who insisted on reminding me at any convenient opportunity, enema insertion or break in the conversation, how lucky I was. There I was, a crumpled bag of bits, lying in abject agony unable to move, pissing fire through a hose pipe, being fed through a piece of the same and being forced to shit once a fortnight into a recycled egg box. To make matters worse I was uncertain if I would ever walk again or regain the use of my arms, if indeed I still had them in the plural, and these people thought that I was lucky. I do not remember my predicament ever being given out as first prize on the Generation game or auctioned off in the raffle at the annual golf club dinner. I figured that I was possibly destined never again to be able to wipe my own arse or even to raise an arm to be taken to the required depository in the first place. In short, I felt about as lucky as the man who after been informed that he had just won 80 million pounds on the lottery was immediately told that his wife had run off with his best mate and the money, and that he had less than twelve hours to live after contracting an acute case of terminal knob rot. I knew exactly how the mayor of Dresden felt after being given the keys to the city, only to find that there were no locks or indeed buildings left following an RAF 'stag do' visit, circa 1945. For sure, from my perspective, I did not share their exaggerated enthusiasm for my survival, whilst their metaphorical glass may always have been half full, mine was lying in a million pieces and was in dire need of some immediate medical intervention, I figured that if ever I was going to be lucky now would be an appropriate place to start.

It took three consultants many hours of head scratching, X rays, MRI scans, blood tests, urine tests, prodding, pulling, poking, etc. before they were able to discover the full extent of my injuries and formulate a game plan to reassemble the broken me. Without resorting to the use of graphic details necessitating a masters degree in Latin and an understanding of advanced surgical procedures, I will attempt to explain the extent of my injuries in 'lay mans terms' a sort of 'Ladybird book of fractures and injuries'. My left arm was paralysed from the shoulder down, this was as a result of it been wrenched from its socket and deposited half way up my arse, the neurones there in, the so called Brachial Plexus, were stretched and torn to such an extent that some of them would never be able to function again. Apparently severe dislocations can do more harm than breakages and take considerably longer to heal than broken bones. To make matters worse, the lower end of my biceps had been ripped away from wherever it is that biceps are supposed to be secured, this did not aid the function of my arm in the least. My neck had been broken in two places, the people in the know spoke of C4,C5,T3,T4 etc., apparently, in the trade these labels refer to the individual segments of the spinal column. I just knew, with a certain degree of accuracy, belying my lack of medical training, that the fucking fucker was fucking fucked and with all probability was going to remain fucking fucked for a fucking long time. Similarly my lower spine was broken in two places, which would necessitate the use of some pretty major welding, plating, drilling and

179

screwing, from this point on I was referred to in certain circles as 'Robopop'. My Trapezoid bone, along with other smaller bones, in my left hand had been, as the consultant explained, turned into dust as a result of me refusing to relinquish my hold on my bloody handle bars, at least my hands unlike many of the residents of Gainsborough, still had the allotted number of digits attached. My right arm resembled an unassembled orthopaedics jigsaw puzzle, most of the pieces appeared to be present but none of them seemed to be in the correct place and worryingly, there appeared to be too many pieces left over. I did not discover the cruellest and most enduring injury until the day of my discharge from hospital, when the offending article was removed. The problem was the result of the on call house doctors inability to insert a catheter into my most tender bits, to be fair the poor sod had only recently left 'prep' school and was in all probability still wanking over his anatomical dictionary. Obviously, he had the intelligence to understand that if I was going to be laid on my back for several months, my body's ability to produce urine was going to cause a not inconsiderable problem for the ward staff, particularly the cleaners. Unfortunately, he was totally incapable of performing this relatively simple task. Instead my wife demonstrated her adeptness with cock tubes and promptly inserted the drain in the appropriate aperture. I suspect in an underhand and unsportsmanlike way of getting even for my previous transgressions, she probably utilized a redundant piece of workman's hose, which was left over from the latest refit, instead of the more regularly used micro bore, rather than securing it in place with a small balloon, in my bladder, I further suspect that she nailed it in place. Fortunately, since I had also ripped out many of my nerves down my back I was unable to feel most of the consequences of her penile delving, the moral of the story is don't piss off the wife when you are not in a position to retaliate, especially when you haven't had a piss for several days. The results of her rudimentary irrigation technique, ensured that the ward was kept clean, dry and odour free, as I dutifully pissed in a plastic bag for weeks on end, the procedure also ensured that I had my own personal hot water bottle available 24 hours a day. Unfortunately, the resultant damage to my best mates internals meant that, to this day, I still piss in two different directions approximately 120 degrees apart, this necessitates the use of the 'sit down' weeing technique which is a whole lot cleaner and more hygienic than the standard male practice, alas it is not as efficient in public urinals where standing alongside me is akin to pissing with a lawn sprinkler with advanced Parkinson's disease, unless that is you happen to be a subscriber to Water sports weekly. I have seriously considered taking clarinet lessons to alleviate the problem, whilst I understand that this will not physically make things better, I hope that I can discover a new fingering technique to cover a few unwanted holes and endeavour to piss in a straight line. One thing is certain, Lady Langdale may be a fully qualified nursing sister but she is most definitely not CORGI registered.

Only the Italians could name a beer after another side effect of my accident, the nerve damage to my lower back resulted in an Ed Miliband like swing to the left in the trouser department, apparently the medical term for this penile disfigurement is Peroni, I kid you not, only the Italians could think of that.

It was round about this juncture of my merry hospital jaunt that it began to dawn on my simple brain that, quite possibly, my hitherto promising modelling career was going to have to be put on hold for the foreseeable future, primarily as a result of my arms not being able to move, since they were hanging off my body, furthermore I had a spinal column like a jelly jenga. It was also readily apparent that my standing as an international ten pin bowling supremo was also going to be adversely affected. Since I was unable to scratch my own arse it seemed reasonably logical that, patently, I would find it damned near impossible to launch a ten pound bowling ball down an alley, even a very short one. In truth, the last time I had three fingers in anything was at the rear of a maths class circa 1976, whilst attempting to recreate my tribute to the stand up puppet legend Sooty, with myself adopting the role of H Corbett and the recipient of my digital invasion being a more than willing 16 year old apprentice nymphet, who was more interested in my rudimentary probing than the relevance of Pi in the modern world. The only pie she had the slightest interest in was her own rather well thumbed, hairy version and its inherent ability to eat schoolboy fingers, unfortunately, for her, I do not recall that being a part of the syllabus circa 1977.

The next time you find yourself considering being ill, it may be in the best interests of your bank account, to think again. For starters you almost certainly cannot afford a spell in the local infirmary, unless that is you happen to be a multimillionaire MP in which case you could claim the cost back on your expenses sheet. If you are not that fortunate, you have a conscience and your local postcode lottery entitles you to have a bed in the local hospital in the first place and your operation is not cancelled at the last nanosecond, due to lack of funding and the fact that some twat spent the budget on new wallpaper and management bonding sessions at a foreign five star hotel, you and your family face a hefty bill for parking. Personally, I struggle with this concept, to me it appears to be just another unstealthy stealth tax. As rate and tax payers we already own the hospital and its grounds, I don't recall, charging myself to park on my driveway at home, another property which similarly, I own. I am certain that an underworked administrator struggling through on one hundred thousand pounds a year salary could explain his reasoning, but I just don't get it.

Since we pay his wages, it stands to reason that we also own him/her, so why not just drown him/her in a bucket of shit and use his/her organs for medical research and dissection. If you are lucky enough to have funds left over from the parking fiasco, you may be able to afford the subsequent prescription fees, although in truth, death is a far cheaper option. Ironically, the Muppets who we pay to make these crass decisions on our behalf, invariably award themselves free private parking bays and benefit from tax payer funded private health care and cars, bring on the revolution!!

Once upon a time our hospital wards had sufficient television sets to go around, these were usually donated by grateful patients and their families in gratitude for their care, or alternatively they were supplied from charitable funds, to make a patients stay in hospital more bearable and to prevent them from finding ceiling tiles interesting, and thus becoming a real pain in the arse at the local pub when they felt the urge to share their extensive knowledge on the subject with the rest of the locals on a Friday night. This system worked well until the health and safety executive in conjunction with various cerebrally challenged administrators, locked all the TVs in a large cupboard somewhere, out of the way, in the basement, and came up with the wizard wheeze of charging the inmates 5 pounds a day for the benefit of getting a closer, high definition picture of the news readers cleavage, inches away from their face, being as they are suspended from the wall behind each individual bed. I still find it difficult to comprehend that the administrator who came up with this organised blackmail did not have parents who were serial wheel clampers and did not come top of the class at geek school, no doubt his next notion will be to kidnap small children with learning difficulties in the hospital foyer and hold them in a dungeon until a ransom demand is paid by their distraught parents.

If you are still intent on being ill, my advice would most definitely be to move to Scotland or Wales, where you will not be charged for the privilege of parking or prescriptions and thus being ill feels like you are getting something for nothing, moreover you will also be able to study for a degree for free during your hospital stay, assuming you do not die of some virulent infection in the meantime, the favourite subject at the moment appears to be 'how to rip off the English', the other obvious alternative would be to get yourself detained in one of her Majesties private hotels, or prisons as I prefer to call them. Obviously, not everybody is lucky enough to be sent to one of these fine establishments, in truth the budding criminal would have to commit a serious, heinous offence to be admitted, nothing soft like a burglary, rape or murder but something really bad, like stepping on a line on the pavement, or overfilling a dustbin by two microns. At least when you do reach your destination it will doubtless have sumptuous warm accommodation and personal care, the food will be edible and the drugs, anal sex and television will be on the house. I cannot help feeling this country has gone sadly wrong on the whole ethics/morals thing, the inevitable result seems to be that most prisoners enjoy their stay in their makeshift holiday homes to such an extent that they cannot wait for a return visit, whilst the pensioners of this green and unpleasant land, who have fought and worked all their lives for the good of their country, are forced to live in relative poverty whilst turning blue from October to March and surviving on tinned cat food. Logic dictates that we, as a society, should swap their respective residences around and everything will surely be tickety-boo, this simple expedient would ensure that our aged and needy are able to live out their days in relative luxury with twenty four hour care and the scum can die alone in their own shit, or is that just too damned simple and politically incorrect?. When we remember that for most people, unlike my dear mother, who has made being ill her life-long hobby and vocation, being sick and needing care is not a lifestyle choice but a necessity, which after all, most patients have contributed towards at some point in their lives (unless they happen to be Romanians or gyppos), it seems wrong that we as a nation should further penalise them when they are at their most vulnerable. Why can't we just get the overpaid, oxygen scavenging administrators, who run the show, to treat patients as human beings and not figures on an account ledger to be erased and manipulated at the slightest opportunity to suit their aspirational targets. If we as a nation really are that strapped for cash that we cannot afford to educate our children or look after our old and needy, here are a few suggestions. Stop sending billions of pounds of taxpayers money that could be spent on the old and sick, to rebel warlords in countries such as Somalia and Rwanda in the form of foreign aid projects, in order that their feral war lords are able to fight their private battles and swan around in private jets and top of the range luxury cars, whilst the locals die of starvation and diarrhoea. Stop sending overseas aid to countries like Pakistan and India who cannot be bothered to look after their own poor, but who, ironically, can afford their own nuclear programmes and space programmes and have the largest number of millionaires on the planet. Stop giving aid to the murderous Chinese who have the fastest growing economy on the planet and one of the worst human rights records to boot, not that it really matters since there are millions of them and in any case they all look the same and they probably deserve their lot for having unpronounceable names and being about as environmentally 'green' as the cheese which grows on the surface of Mars. Most importantly, get rid of the overpaid bureaucratic pyramid building administrators and box tickers who came up with these ridiculous ideas in the first place. Perhaps then our most vulnerable would not be forced to spend their twilight days alone in a dark hospital corridor or forced to lie in their own shit and survive on boiled cabbage soup, whilst admiring their new collection of bruises and ulcers in some third rate extortionately priced nursing home. To compound the misery, in order too be admitted into this lonely transit camp to the undertakers, the resident will undoubtedly have had to sell their house, dentures, soul and the odd kidney or two, to pay for the privilege and to assist the owner of the joint in the purchase of his new waterside mansion in Marbella and a new Ferrari. Somehow, I do not think that the government's doling out of winter fuel allowance will help our cold, hungry pensioners in any way other than easing the guilt of the parasites at the top. I cannot help feeling that in Britain today it is better to live off the state and gamble, smoke or piss away any assets before the onset of old age, rather than be prudent and industrious, just a thought! My what a contumacious old twat I have become.

Being of an inherently tight nature, I refused to pay the extortionate daily rental fee to watch the daytime rantings of the likes of Jerry Springer and Richard and Judy, an ill conceived idea at the best of times, but when the viewer is unable to switch that women's wizened face off when it is presented in high definition, approximately twelve inches from the end of ones nose, disapproval will inevitably turn to outright fear, even through a morphine induced mist. Instead I preferred the cheaper option of my continued appreciation of the ceiling and allowed my battered brain cells to cogitate as to why an inordinate number of nursing staff who quite frankly should have known better, were grossly obese and appeared to cultivate 'bingo wings' and chin stubble for a hobby, in no way did the majority of the NHS angels measure up to my adolescent cravings for uniforms and role play sessions, maybe I should have gone private after all.

I've often considered that I would make a first class copper, I knew I had all the basic attributes required for the job. Firstly, I would gladly sell my own mother, without batting an eye lid, in exchange for a couple of pieces of silver and, secondly, I am rudely arrogant and about as bent as my own, post accident extremely, bent member. Never one to stand, or in my case lay, idly by when confronted by crime, in full view of my slightly blurred eyes, I set about the task of bringing law and order to the ward. I had observed for several nights that something was most definitely amiss each time that the night shift came on duty and the ward fell quiet for the evening. As the lights dimmed the local drug barons activities began. In order too frustrate his trade in human misery, I related my observations and worries to Lady Langdale. I explained that the large black guy with the dreadlocks was the one selling the drugs to all manner of undesirable junkies and addicts, especially the low life who climbed through the window behind my bed each evening to obtain his fix. I further explained to my wife that I feared for my safety and that this corrupt trade had to be stopped. She in turn explained that the drug baron was in fact the Charge Nurse doing his evening drug rounds, with the other staff, and that it was highly improbably that anybody could enter the building via the window in question by virtue of the fact that a) the person accused would have to be a very agile dwarf since the window was only six inches wide and b) the ward was situated some six stories from the ground. Since apparently Alain Robin does not have an 18inch high, free climbing, dwarfish love child, the whole concept seemed somewhat unfeasible, as apparently did my assertion that the same window was where the mice that danced on the ceiling each evening, entered the building. Bloody good stuff that Morphine, although in truth it works best when the user in question is slightly unstable in the first place.

Narcotics dealing is one thing, but cold blooded murder is another altogether more serious subject. Unless that is it involves strangling small screaming unruly and uncontrollable infants on budget airline flights of anything over thirty minutes duration, who frankly ought to have been removed from the gene pool via the simple expedient of cot death. So it was that I became the unwilling witness of such a crime carried out on the little old lady in the adjacent bed. Her poor fragile frame stood little chance against the gang of hoodlums who precipitated her death. Whilst some of the baying crowd held her down, the ringleader held the Tesco carrier bag over her aged head until she became motionless and her struggles subsided, in her case every little bit did not help one iota. I again related the incident to Lady Langdale, who after discussion with the ward sister, again related to me that I was talking bollocks and that the carrier bag in question, i.e. the murder weapon, was in fact a portable oxygen tent to assist the ladies laboured breathing. The sister, on hearing my allegations, simply laughed them off and explained that since the lady in question was a wealthy private patient, the last thing the hospital would do was to bring about her untimely demise, especially as they needed a new extension to the ward with the requisite equipment and funding. She did however concede that the lady had in fact died, a point which pleased me immensely, since my next allegation would have been that I had witnessed her been eaten by a large 8 foot long black plastic caterpillar with a zip down its back and wheels where its legs should have been, that assertion would quite obviously have made me look like a total and complete twat. More morphine please nurse!

During the ensuing weeks, the surgeons took turns at welding, plating and sewing what was left of my bones, muscles and nerves back together. Some operations were relatively short, being of a couple hours duration, the longest involved the stabilization of my spine and took the best part of the day, together with many needles and a fair few reels of thread, by the time they had finished with me I looked like a well used teddy bear which was obviously past saving, but had been in the family that long that they could not bring themselves to throw it out with the rest of the shit. Following cataract surgery some years ago even my eyes are now plastic, which only serves to strengthen the comparison, it would appear that with each passing year my ageing body increasingly resembles the Cutty Sark, in so much as there is precious little of the original me left, unlike the famous tea clipper however it is debatable whether the accountants of the NHS would have spent fifty million quid to save me. As a result of the abundance of scars which now traverse my back, neck and arms, my body now resembles an aerial relief map of the fields and hedgerows of rural England.

Understandably I was not best pleased when two weeks later I was hurriedly returned to theatre to be unceremoniously unzipped and have the festering infection that was consuming my body from the inside out, washed out with copious amounts of Dettol, brick acid and antibiotics. A cynic would no doubt assert that this was necessary because the administrators had deemed it more important to waste millions of pounds on new wallpaper and furniture to make their homely little pyramids more comfortable, than to invest a few groats on cleaning staff and the requisite materials with which to accomplish the task. If they had opted for the latter, the chances are that the same filthy dressing which had taken up residence under my bed would not have lain, there as it did, incubating its filth, for over a week. Quite simply a few pounds spent on simple hygiene and cleanliness would undoubtedly save millions in theatre time, drugs and staff hours, not to mention a whole lot of pain, discomfort and heartache for the patients, thanks a lot you underworked, overpaid bunch of box ticking, degree toting cunts!

By the end of my sojourn to hell, the anaesthetists had run out of veins to extract my blood or fill me with whatever drugs were on the menu for the day. I used to dread the sound of the phlebotomists footsteps coming down the ward corridor, unfortunately there are only a limited number of hiding places in a 6 foot by 3 foot bed, especially when its resident is unable to move. During the last operation, which I was forced to endure, the anaesthetists, resorted to using my jugular vein as a doorway to my inner self, since all the usual entrance points had dropped off, healed over, or like a bent politician whose fraudulent expenses have been discovered, gone deep under cover, this was after and probably because I informed them that, the last time I had seen it, there was a large blue vein down the outside of my cock, which they were welcome to use if it would make their task any easier, they ignored my comments and I woke up some hours later with a sore neck, still, could have been a lot worse I guess!

By the end of my communal Meccano session I was the proud new owner of four long titanium rods and sixteen nuts and bolts down my spine, together with two plates and twelve bolts down my right arm, my left arm remained paralysed. Considering the current scrap value of Colorado titanium a walk by the local vermin enclosure of the resident scrap dealing fraternity, who I am told prefer the term traveller despite the fact that they have not travelled further than the local DSS office for a very long time, became a whole lot more exciting, not to mention brisk. On one occasion, as I came round from a particularly harrowing operation. I was busy mentally thanking Steve Austin for his pioneering work in the field of body welding and robotics, which had undoubtedly helped to save my life and dignity, when I was woken by my wives voice. Following my latest operation, I had been in theatre recovery for some considerable time as a result of my sky high blood pressure, even in my semi-comatose state I was apparently still capable of making a total prat of myself. My wife informed me that the recovery ward nurse was called Norma, to which I, in my inimitable way enquired if her surname was Stitz or Scunt for sure it was only the drips, wires and drains in my body which saved me from receiving a swift clip around the ear from Lady Langdale and in all probability the nurse herself, fortunately I never got to met the nurses twin sister Gloria. I rarely slept during my two months in hospital partly because of the constant pain, but, principally because each time I fell asleep the nursing staff would wake me, either to see if I was asleep, which clearly I was, or to turn me in order to prevent the development of bed sores, to give me drugs to make me sleep or to take what was left of my blood or seemingly just to wake me up for the sake of it. Vindictive bastards those nurses, I know, I have been married to one for thirty bloody years, in the observers dictionary of nursing the word sympathy comes somewhere between shit and syphilis.

In truth, the only thing in hospital to look forward to is the morning bed bath, that and going home hopefully in a better state than when admitted and without a serious bacterial/viral infection. On one occasion, I was being bathed by an attractive looking blonde nurse who enquired if it was alright to wash the bits which, pre accident, I had usually washed myself at whatever speed I deemed necessary, when I replied that she could 'fill her boots' and take as long as she liked since I normally had to pay for such pleasures, she promptly squeezed the contents of her hands, i.e. my bollocks in a wholly uncomfortable, unprofessional and inappropriate manner for a young lady of her calling ,whilst smiling profusely. I could envisage the same young lady blowing up an inflatable dingy or air bed in the same manner, after this encounter, strangely I always got the fat ugly nurses, with personal hygiene problems and excessive facial hair, to carry out my ablutions.

Since I rarely slept, I become the unofficial designated sentry on guard for the other inmates, who, for whatever reason were unable to look after themselves. The poor man in the neighbouring bed had undergone a hip replacement operation, unfortunately, since he had contracted MRSA, which was apparently 'a la mode' on the ward, the artificial joint had had to be removed. This meant that essentially nothing now held his leg to his body and he was therefore rendered, immobile, this also caused untold troubles for his aged waterworks and plumbing systems, frequently he would shout the nurses for assistance , but invariably, since they were short staffed or eating biscuits, his cries for help would go unanswered or invariably they would arrive just in time to see his most authentic imitation of Rome's Trevi fountain or occasionally a Sumatran mud slide depending on which way he was facing at the time, as with most of us his dignity was left at reception on admission.

For much of my life, but more so as I have become older and more cynical, I have been a devout atheist, especially since the Bigman's apparent amusement and entertainment at my expense involving his pain threshold tests with my bones and testicles, which only served to strengthen my beliefs, or lack of them. My lack of conviction was further reinforced when I realised that the bosses name was merely dog spelled backwards, whilst I have a lot of affection for my canine companion, I have never felt the urge to idolise her or start a war on her behalf, particularly since she spends a lot of time licking her own genitals and eating her own vomit. Ever since I was old enough to watch TV or read a newspaper, I became aware of one indisputable fact about religion, i.e. that it causes more wars, bloodshed and heartache than any other factor on the planet, with the possible exception of mans greed and his craving for oil and women's damp bits. Unlike some people I have never found comfort in religion, maybe it is simply because the idea of having a hypocritical priests rampant member thrust up my poo hole at choir practice just never really appealed, especially whilst the culprit insisted on telling me, what a bad Christian and member of society I was, just because of the discovery of one bloody porn magazine in an RE lesson years ago. When will these deviant ambassadors of uphill gardening realise that anal sex is very similar too spinach and Brussels sprouts, if it is forced on the unwilling recipient during early childhood, there is a very good chance that they are not going to enjoy it later on in life.

As a natural cynic, I never believed the advertising pamphlets and manifestos of the World's religious movements, even as a child, all the bullshit about virgin births didn't wash with me, I reasoned with a certain degree of accuracy, that if I had tried to use the same excuse when arriving home pissed, and announced to Lady Langdale that our fourteen year old babysitter had conceived as a result of an immaculate conception, I would be in A and E or the divorce courts before I could say hail Mary, most probably carrying my wedding tackle in a carrier bag. She most certainly would not be hammering on the church door in a hurry to praise the Lord and 'big up' his wayward son. I further reasoned that I would have similar problems when I tried to convince the girl's parents, the judge and the jury, especially if the latter included a few would be Germaine Greers and equal opportunities lesbians. The turning water into wine affair is also beset with inherent shortcomings, although I am able to perform the trick the opposite way round with some gusto, bizarrely, even then, I am told it tastes better than Liebfraumilch. By the time we get to the few stale loaves and a tin of John West sardines chapter, if it was that easy, some philanthrope who didn't waste his time trying to walk on water and wasn't daft enough to end their days nailed to a couple of vertical railway sleepers, would undoubtedly have solved the problem of world starvation decades ago, personally I think our mutual redeemer was simply bullshitting in a half hearted attempt at getting a shag and impressing the birds.

Just how big did Noah build his arc in order that he could fit on board two of every living creature, even P&O cattle class would struggle with that one. Even if he had had the foresight to keep his selection to just insects, I reckon that he would need a vessel about the size of the QE2, until that is, the residents started eating each other, even accounting for the reproductive abilities of flies and locusts, one bloke building a vessel large enough to accommodate them all, is still a difficult concept to grasp. The problem becomes more unbelievable if we consider that he had a woman to help him, imagine the arguments that that error of judgement would have caused. If we throw the mammals, reptiles and larger fauna into the equation, then the vessel required would presumably be approximately the size of Europe. How on earth is one man and his belligerent wife going to clean up that amount of shit, even if they simply threw it overboard and in so doing established America, it is still a far fetched concept to grasp. Admittedly, the work load would diminish as the inmates gradually ate each other and were ravished by kennel cough, and in so doing, left just the higher order carnivores and the odd snake, but I still don't buy the lack of logic, by the end of the voyage, some 40 nights I'm reliably lead to believe, the ship would undoubtedly have bore more than a passing resemblance to a Somalian zoo at famine time, i.e. empty. God, in

199

his infinite wisdom, although if Noah was his best shot it doesn't seen that infinite to me, apparently caused all this death and destruction to us mortals, to show how much he loved man kind and promised he would never hurt us again, until the two world wars inconveniently came along at any rate. Obviously, I am paraphrasing, but presumably you get my point, even at this early stage in his career, God, seemingly, was a nasty bastard.

When it comes to religion, I most definitely am a non-believer there are undoubtedly areas of the subject of which I profess to be less certain. I am, for example, a great believer in fate, no matter how bad a situation or event may at first appear, with the passing of time and the benefit of hindsight, I usually find everything has a reason and results in some unforeseen benefits at the end of the day. Eventually, I even found this to be the case with my horrific accident and resultant injuries and disabilities, if nothing else I believe my experience made me a better, more compassionate, person and gave me a second shot at life, and I got my bollocks played with for free. I would not for one minute suggest that these views are in any way religious, nor would I try to impose them on someone else, in short, I believe that there are many things that we do not understand and thus I try, whenever possible, to keep an open mind, so long as it doesn't involve dress wearing deviants and botty action in the vestry on a Sunday morning. One such incident which leads me to keep an 'open mind' on matters which I do not understand, occurred during my internment in hospital. Walt was an elderly man of quiet character who ordinarily had very little to say, rather, he preferred to sit and dribble and grind his teeth, apparently he had no living family and very few visitors. In between my ceiling tile observations, occasionally we would strike up a limited conversation which was usually interspersed with the odd drug fuelled rant and compulsory disorientation and resultant expletives and spillages. One evening, from out of the blue, Walt announced to the ward that he was going to die on Monday, apparently that's when 'they' were coming for him, although he didn't give an exact time, or disclose what form of transport he was planning to use, in his mind, or rather what was left of it, he was convinced of the accuracy of his prediction. Whilst at the time his assertion seemed a little peculiar, since he was still breathing at regular intervals, nonetheless, during the course of the weekend his health progressively declined and Walt, slipped into a comatose state, even his teeth grinding had ceased, now the only noise which passed his lips was the odd grunt or moan. I was awoken in the early hours from a welcome and rare nap, to see the usually horizontal Walt pinned against the head board of his bed in a distorted kneeling position, seemingly held there by some unearthly, invisible force, not bad for a man who had not even sat up for a week. The fear in his voice was all too apparent, as his aging arms thrashed around in a vain attempt to repel his unseen assailants. The last words Walt ever spoke on this planet were that 'they had come for him' and that 'he didn't want to go,' like a small child he pleaded with his attackers to leave him alone. I summoned the nurses who dutifully called the 'crash team', by the time that they had arrived, Walt lay silent and crumpled, although he still excelled on the dribbling front, despite their best efforts Walt's prophecy had indeed being fulfilled, he never regained consciousness. It was Monday night, just as Walt had predicted. Now, in my book, that is proper religion, no fear of burning in hell, eternal damnation or oppression from a man in a frock who is pissed out of his head on cheap communion wine and cracking one off in the confession box over last month's edition of 'War cry', and no bum loving sexual predators for miles around.

Wilf resided in the bed by the window, the man had single handedly perfected the wholly unsocial practice of leaving a Hansel and Gretel like trail of shit from his bed to the toilet, situated some distance, across the ward. He spent much of his day practising oral macramé with snot candles which festooned his nostrils, in a perpetual cycle of production and ingestion, his nasal contortions reminded me of the belt on an old threshing machine, constantly thrashing about to feed the machine. I wondered at what point the thixotropic goo would fly off the axle and plaster the rest of his face with his nasal oozings. Little wonder that the ceiling tiles held such fascinations when this was the alternative entertainment on offer, still they made Channel four look like good TV. Wilf's other hobby was being rude and obnoxious to the staff and inmates, he excelled in this particular discipline and spent many hours practising and honing his all too apparent abilities in the field, frequently he would attempt to better his own impressive record for the highest number of arguments in one day, his dedication in the field of ignorance and cuntdom was legendary.

Whilst the man in the adjoining bed was doing his utmost to die from a sudden bout of heart stoppingness, Wilf decided that, that moment was appropriate to gatecrash the party, which by now consisted of approximately a dozen doctors and nurses of the resuscitation team, and enquire as to where his dinner was. Apparently, the answer for which he was hoping was not forth coming , and so Wilf pressed home his verbal attack by enquiring 'why is he more important than me'?. I resisted the temptation to say 'because he is fucking dying you inconsiderate snot eating twat, now get back into your bed and be quite', instead I decided on the safer and somewhat more entertaining option of quietly watching the melee unfold. Similarly the doctor holding the defibrillator apparently resisted the temptation to insert the paddles up Wilf's arse and give it maximum voltage, although in truth the rancid paste which was now spread across his face, would undoubtedly have made a better target and more conductive medium for the machines current. Instead, the staff just pretended Wilf wasn't there, with all the decorum of a violinist on the Titanic at sinking time, even when he stuck his head through the curtains and shouted ' never mind him, where's my fucking dinner' he was still ignored., What to Wilf was a perfectly reasonable question, was repeated at greater levels of volume and increased rapidity, unfortunately, his ever more frantic attempts did little to precipitate the answer for which Wilf was searching and indeed, in his own stubborn way expected, as a matter of courtesy. Eventually, he returned to his bed and proceeded to attempt to eat the contents of a sputum bowl which was full of cold sick, and which in the words of the best chefs, 'he had prepared earlier'. Unfortunately, his chosen implement, i.e. a fork was of little use in the operation and so once again the contents of the bowl were spread across his chin and beard, maybe there is a God after all, although with the benefit of hindsight his choice of sustenance may not have been as strange as first impressions would suggest, given the quality of hospital meals, and their inherent lack of nutrients. I sincerely hope that the authorities keep this man's brain after his demise or indeed before, if they see fit, by comparing it to a working modern day version perhaps scientists will at last be able to ascertain why certain members of the human race feel the urge to watch inane dross such as Big Brother and The X Factor on their television screens, and in so doing consign the talentless entities thereon to seek gainful employment removing entrails in a chicken factory.

Perhaps it was the sight of Wilf's makeshift snack which turned my stomach or maybe just the excitement of the moment, but turn it did in a wholly inconvenient way in which it had not turned for approximately two weeks. Alas, none of my medical team had bothered to inform me, or their fellow colleagues, it would appear, of the constipational effects of morphine, especially when taken by the bucket full, as I was doing. Granted, without its pain relieving abilities I would have been in a state, but at least my lower alimentary canal would not have become as congested as the M25 on a Friday evening. It would appear that all the excitement on the ward had acted as a bizarre form of visual laxative, the result being that my body decided that this was an appropriate time to evacuate two weeks' worth of shit. Unfortunately, my arse had different ideas regarding the work in hand, it lulled my colon into a false sense of relief before clamping firmly shut on what could best be described as a six inch wide endless turd of synthetic 'shitcrete,' the surface of which was seemingly embedded with rusty nails and old razor blades. Since my body was still in several disconnected pieces and I was laid prone, i.e. on my back, I found the whole procedure, to say the least, challenging. Unlike the more normal and accepted way of defecating, which I have to say, with the benefit of experience, is a whole lot more efficient and comfortable, this method was not only incredibly painful but sadly disappointing in the production department, in truth it was like trying to pass an obese hedgehog, which had, as a result of some unfortunate accident become smothered with superglue, uphill through a balloon pool, i.e. painful and futile. Whilst the turtles metaphorical head was indeed protruding from its burrow, its legs were firmly stuck, furthermore there was no way it was coming out to play. It was at this juncture of the proceedings that the doctors and nurses decided that it would make the night shift pass a little quicker if they were to stuff every type of enema and suppository, in their extensive arsenal, simultaneously up my posterior aperture, in order to facilitate the birth of the stubborn bum baby. I am sure that I observed the ward sister taking side bets on the outcome as the rest of the crew gathered around with a stopwatch and gawped at my aching sphincter and it's overly shy resident, whilst waiting for the fireworks to start. Unfortunately, their heroic efforts proved to be in vain, despite clouds of acrid smoke, a few sparks and a modicum of seepage, Tommy Turtle, as my bum hole baby had been christened most definitely was not going to the ball.

I am reliably informed that the authorities, in partnership no doubt with the Health and Safety executive, had dictated that nursing staff are no longer allowed to perform the procedure known as 'manual evacuation', whilst this may sound like the name of a dyslexic Spanish flatulence champion, it does actually refer to the technique of shoving a finger, spade, crowbar or whatever else is at hand up a patients arse, in order to remove the blockage therein. This procedure used to be a part of every nurses training but now the authorities have deemed that it is better to leave the patients to suffer in abject agony and do fuck all, something at which they are apparently very good, since they do it on a daily basis for long periods of time. I bet that the monthly meeting of administrators, with this motion on the agenda was an interesting one, with the spokesperson announcing a motion about motions or rather the lack of them. The outcome of these deliberations is that it is no longer acceptable for staff to stick their fingers up a patients arse in order to remove stubborn clinker. If only the priesthood could come up with a similar mandate, life would be so much easier, and undoubtedly less painful, for the average choirboy.

Fortunately, I had my own resident and fully qualified anal probing shit remover at hand, when Lady Langdale dully appeared wearing an elbow length pair of latex gloves and a large smile which was somewhat akin to a sadistic deviant vet on horse tranquilizers, the nursing sister on duty decided that now would be an opportune time to ignore this pathetic piece of management legislation and get on with the job, or jobs in hand. Two minutes later, I was laid on my side whilst being anally violated and roughly probed in an attempt too remove the blockage, had I not been in such pain and in a hospital environment, this procedure may have been a whole lot more pleasurable than it appeared at the time.

Being a confirmed pessimist my thoughts at the time were that the next point of contact would be 'Dynorod', a concept on which I did not wish to dwell for more time than was absolutely necessary.

At least now I can hold my own in conversations with mothers who insist that the male of the species does not understand the pain of childbirth, believe me, having four above average sized fingers and a head sized piece of shitcrete hanging out of ones arse tends to focus the mind. From there on in, I made certain that whenever a doctor prescribed morphine I got the complimentary gift box of laxatives in order to prevent a rerun of that unforgettable night. Whilst it seemed that this procedure may be an effective deterrent for rapists and the average child molester come 'kiddy fiddler', it seemed wholly inappropriate to a wimp like me with an inherent morbid fear of pain, I most certainly do not have any plans either to repeat the whole fisting thing anytime soon or indeed to become friends with Mary and attempt a spot of uphill gardening. Fortunately, for me and my innards the anal probings paid off and normal service was resumed without recourse to a high pressure water hose, alas it also precipitated a shortage of bed pans with the staff running around like headless chickens trying to juggle too many plates and remove the resulting residue. Without doubt on a conventional toilet I would have been touching water and laying cable for a considerable length of time, the resultant fallout would have been above high water mark, resembling as it did, a slightly smaller and downmarket vision of Dubai's Berge Tower.

The date was July 1st, as usual Lady Langdale arrived for her daily visit to the funny farm. She explained that she had had to run the gauntlet of protesters at the hospitals main entrance who were objecting to the governments and hospitals new strict no smoking regulations, which prevented, amongst other things, smoking in the hospital grounds. Whilst admirable in its attempt to try and save money for us hard up smokers, although the government insist they are trying to save our lungs and lives, all that the legislation appears to have accomplished, is to instigate the mass migration of smokers to the perimeter road in their nighties, pyjamas and slippers duly following by a multitude of catheter bags, drip stands and heart monitors in order too set up base camp on the pavement. Unfortunately, the pavement was invariably contaminated with every germ known to man, and this being Sheffield, no doubt some more that weren't, since it was festooned with half eaten kebabs and piles of dog shit and sick with the inevitable slipper foot print embossed therein. Surely, even a retarded lobotomy patient could see that such a policy would only encourage the spread of infection and disease throughout the hospital, when those same patients returned. No amount of antiseptic alcohol gels on ward entrances is going to make the slightest difference, unless that is, the staff systematically strip each person and fully immerse their bodies in a vat of the stuff and burn all their clothes and slippers each time they go out for a smoke. Many smokers simply ignored the rules and threats of conviction and continued to light up in the doorways and entrances, seemingly oblivious to the new Day-Glo notices adorning the walls and windows. Frankly, judging by the oxygen masks and depleted number of limbs in evidence, I would imagine that a fine for smoking another fag was the very least of their worries. It did however strike a chord of irony that the freedom for which the protesters were fighting was probably the reason that they were there in the first place, due to the adverse effects of smoking, circulation problems and lung cancer, still on a lighter note, apparently the wheelchair manufacturers were doing a roaring trade.

I recall on one occasion the tedium of daily life on the ward was relieved by the arrival of a new inmate. Unusually, this one had a brain and was able to converse, although for reasons that later became clear he accomplished this feat via the corner of his mouth, like a Down's syndrome sufferer who had suffered a stroke. Glyn was a fireman whose crew had been called out on an 'emergency mission'. The emergency was caused by a hard of thinking cat who was doing what cats do best, i.e., climbing up something in order to kill it, shit on it or shag it. Unfortunately, some equally retarded member of the public spotted poor tiddles dilemma and decided, as members of the public do, that the cat needed rescuing. To make matters worse tiddles decided to get himself stuck on an asbestos roof, which poor Glyn, on his mercy mission, promptly fell through and plummeted forty feet to the ground below. Presumably, in an attempt to hike his compensation claim, he managed to accomplish his descent by bouncing off various brick walls and obstacles on the way down. The result of his impromptu gymnastics was a punctured lung, a multitude of broken ribs, a broken jaw and various fractures to his shoulder and arms. Oh, how we laughed about it afterwards, whilst he was busy attempting to suck his dinner through a straw. This explained his unusual method of speech, since, what was left of his jaw bone had been wired together to assist its healing. If only Relate would have the balls to pioneer this type of therapy for wives, think how many marriages would be saved. Despite his injuries, Glyn, conceded that in a hospital version of 'Top Trumps', he could not rival my 'spec sheet' for the seriousness, number and size of injuries, implants and scars, despite his obvious discomfort, he would always be the also ran in that particular contest.

Amazingly, Glyn left hospital in a little over a week, but not before his bed had been surrounded by fire service top brass and union officials, who were collectively shitting themselves for fear of law suits, compensation claims and litigation, since it was fairly apparent that his fire fighting days were over and he would spend the rest of his life living on his payout and kicking cats. As Glyn was about to leave the ward and go home, I beckoned him to my bedside, 'Glyn' I said, 'there's something I have been meaning to ask you since the day you arrived, what happened to the cat?' Glyn duly smiled through his wires and considered his response, whilst casting a cursory glance at his various bandages and casts. Slowly and begrudgingly he replied 'the fucking thing climbed through an open window and fucked off never to be seen again', before asserting that he hoped the ginger bastard had by now had an intimate relationship with the rapidly moving north end of a south bound tram. Presumably, he wished the same retribution on the instigator of the 999 call who was responsible for his predicament.

Similarly, I had never particularly considered myself to be an ardent lover of the feline species, as with most creations of nature, with the possible exceptions of tape worms and pubic lice, I would never knowingly go out of my way to cause one pain or suffering. I am the sort of person who would resist the consuming temptation to drive a three wheeled car for fear of flattening the worlds most unlucky hedgehog, for sure it would be just my luck to cave the poor unfortunate's skull in with my ill sited radial, whilst he was busy crossing the road on the way home from hedgehog school and diligently obeying his parents primary rules of road safety, i.e. aim between the wheels.

Perhaps, it is the thought of the little feline fuckers shitting around the house in oversize paint roller trays filled with porridge oats, that I find a mental barrier to cat ownership, furthermore, I would consider it prudent, if not essential, to extract it's talons by means of a pair of pliers as a precaution to prevent it from damaging objects i.e. me. Despite these drawbacks, I have often considered the possibility of having a ginger pussy around the house to occupy the long winter nights, but the thought of having a cat never crossed my mind. Obviously, I never discussed my thoughts with Lady Langdale, principally in the interests of keeping a close relationship with my bollocks and secondly, after my suggestion that I wouldn't object to having an older coloured bird around the house, left me nursing an arthritic African Grey parrot which suffered from acute angina and vertigo attacks, hence it spent most of its time falling off its perch and laying around on sandpaper, this had the added determent of abrading most of its feathers, not really the sort of bald exotic bird which I desired, be careful what you wish for.

I have always found Vegans by their nature a little obscure, for some time now it has crossed my mind that a little intensive therapy to the genre would not go a miss. A good friend of mine, who is a leading exponent of the art, has a serious cat addiction, that is when she is not busy, saving the planet, hugging trees and eating root vegetables and pulses, with all the inherent flatulence involved therein. Despite the fact that her feline pride and joy insisted on killing any living thing, including my legs, within a large radius, in flagrant violation of the Vegan bible, she loved the horrible flea ridden thing. She spent a small fortune on installing a cat flap in her new and expensive door to enable tiddles to go out raping and murdering whenever he wanted. Unfortunately, this turned out to be an open invitation to the other cats in the neighbourhood to drop in for tea whenever they wished, whilst visiting they apparently deemed it polite to scratch the newly installed three piece suite and soft furnishings at their leisure and spray the contents of their arse glands across the carpet in the feline equivalent of an olfactory 'kilroy woz ere' piece of bum graffiti. In a vain attempt to stop the evening pussy raves she fitted her cat, and its associated cat flap, with a state of the art magnetic lock which would only allow entry to her cat, the problem was cured and peace was restored. Until that is, the poor feline decided to go to bed, as with many cat lovers, my friend was not all there, she was a sandwich short of a picnic. Although obviously being a vegan a sandwich, containing no butter, milk, cheese, ham, beef, chicken, honey, eggs etc so just the marmite and cucumber in effect, not really a full sandwich at all then, in truth, just like it's creator.

The problem occurred principally because she insisted on spoiling the little mouser rotten, not for vegan tiddles the normality of a floor based cushion type bed design, instead she installed a high rise cat hammock which sat some three feet up the wall perched on top of the radiator. Presumably, these contraptions are designed to keep puss warm at night, not that I ever recall seeing them being used by mountain lions in the Rockies at sub minus 40c temperatures. Furthermore, I think that her objection to my assertion that placing tiddles in the microwave on full power for 2 minutes would have had the same result and saved some money, was just being plain pedantic. The high tech sleeping system appeared to work in a satisfactory manner until one day, on her return, she observed that tiddles had not eaten his breakfast and was not around to greet her in the usual gouged ankles sort of way. Further investigation revealed the problem, since said cat was now living the high life complete with a large magnetic necklace, the poor little fucker had inadvertently attached itself, via its neck jewellery, to the steel body of the radiator. It was rendered unable to move, with its legs flailing around, third degree burns down its back and a forlorn expression on its 'wob eyed 'feline mug. Good job that the little bird killer had another eight lives.

I recall once sitting on the patio of a sun soaked taverna in Portugal, waiting to order dinner, when I became, not to put too fine a point on it, intrigued by the appearance of a five legged cat. The animal promptly sat down and tried in vain to chew off its rearmost leg, at this point I realised that its extra appendage, its 'arse leg' for the sake of argument, was actually the remains of a plastic bag which was now hanging limply from the first hole from the back of its neck. Presumably, the hungry moggy had devoured the same at the other end without bothering to remove its contents first, in so doing it had inadvertently metamorphosed into a four legged sausage maker. I discussed with Lady Langdale various methods of extricating the blockage and alleviating the animals suffering, before opting for what, on reflection, was possibly the most inhumane, although most efficacious solution, I could have ever concocted, that's what red wine does to my brain. My master plan involved planting my size nine on the offending article, the bag that is not the cat, and then promptly getting down on all fours behind the unsuspecting animal and barking as loud as a half pissed middle aged idiot abroad could possibly accomplish. Much to the consternation and disbelief of my fellow diners, my cunning plan worked a treat, 'Bag Puss' as he was now christened, for obvious reasons, promptly shot forward through the legs of a neighbouring table with a startled expression of incredulity on its face and in the process left behind the offending bag, the previous days breakfast and if I was not mistaken an unknown quantity of entrails, although my mission was swiftly accomplished, my trainers were never the same again. I venture to suggest that the peroxide blonde lady from Essex, who by this point was busy depositing her recently eaten dinner via her mouth and nostrils around the terracotta pot containing a Bougainville, would likewise be mentally scarred for life. Meanwhile, her husband glowered at me in disgust and in a manner which at no point suggested that he was about to invite me round for cocktails and a 'sportsman's double' with his wife. Unsurprisingly, during the rest of our stay we did not venture back to the taverna to see how puss and his prolapsed rectum or the weak stomached blonde were recuperating following their somewhat traumatic experience. That's cat ownership for you!

After several months of ceiling tile appreciation and ridicule, my vacation courtesy of the National Health Service came to an unexpected and abrupt end. To this day I am uncertain if my release from incarceration was as a result of the NHS running out of money, given that the world price of Titanium had gone through the roof, probably as a direct result of the vast quantities which my broken body had consumed. Alternatively, it may simply have been a case of the nursing staff's patience running out, or more probably, that in an unguarded moment whilst no one was looking I ran out. The latter however, seems unlikely since, as I became only too aware the first time that I attempted to stand, the body's muscles begin to atrophy rapidly if not used regularly. Since I had not been out of my bed for some two months, my muscles were apparently in the latter stages of acute anorexia and were as wasted as a Gainsborough crack addict on a Friday night, like most of the country they had packed in the whole working idea many weeks previous. My feeble attempts at walking resembled those of an aging inebriated blancmange with learning difficulties, although I was used to seeing this phenomenon in the pub during most weekends I seemingly managed to accomplish the feat without the introduction of falling down juice, or alcohol, as it more usually referred.

Meanwhile, the ward sister, not content with the physical and mental trauma she had administered with her fisting prowess, decided to rip out the balloon which had secured the catheter in my bladder for some two months, seemingly to observe the excruciating pain thus administered and panic on my face as she roughly man handled my 'pan handle'. The concept of giving birth to a large piece of clinical apparatus (all things are relative) via my somewhat smaller urethra, was not one which I wished to consider for any length of time, or indeed to repeat at any point in the near future. Perhaps the whole operation would have been made a whole lot easier and less painful if the rubber glove wearing sadist had taken the time to even partially deflate the device, as per the instruction manual, at the onset of hostilities.

Once the mobile portaloo was rendered redundant, I had to accomplish the whole urination procedure the way that nature intended, this caused a whole lot more anxiety and consternation on my part. Firstly, the only toilet was located some 20 miles away at the entrance to the ward, at least that is how far it appeared to be since my legs refused to cooperate with the rest of my nervous system. Secondly, my left arm was still paralysed and my right was essentially dead and hanging on by a few nuts and bolts, and was simply there to make the whole thing look balanced and pretty, to compound the situation it was wrapped in a multitude of dressings and fixed in a sling, thus I had no means of pointing Percy replete with a 90' bend, at the porcelain. Thirdly, even if I had been able to complete the three day march to the latrines and performed an incident free splashdown, the chances are that Wilf would have been there first and smeared the cubicle with shit in a continuation of his dirty protest, precipitated by, in his eyes at least, his lack of sustenance and care.

Despite my protestations that I was unable to piss correctly and therefore was a danger to myself and those around me, the authorities in their infinite wisdom, had decided that I was 'persona non gratia' and that I was going, no matter what. This decision probably was a result of Lady Langdale being less the 'Lady with the lamp' and more the 'Lady with the acerbic tongue and letters after her name' it appeared that the staff were more frightened of her than I was, in truth they probably wanted me out of the way before I contracted MRSA, which by now was spreading through the hospital like wildfire. Before I was released from captivity into the wilds of Sheffield, I was obliged to undergo an assessment at the underground torture chamber with the code name 'Occupational Therapy'. My guess is that the staff here had been on an SS day release course, whilst they didn't actually rip my finger nails out, possibly because the financial cut backs had resulted in a shortage of pliers, they administered every other type of torture imaginable to the average unable bodied victim. Since they made it pretty apparent that if I was unable to complete the imminent assault course and torture session I would not be freed, I decided to give it my best. I therefore struggled to complete the climbing of the specially fabricated wooden steps, doors and furniture, although I drew a line at attempting the swinging rope bridge suspended two hundred foot above the raging river and rapids below, and opted instead for the boiling the kettle and making a cup of tea section of the syllabus. Whilst, this may seem to have been the easy option, you try accomplishing the task whilst only being able to use your teeth. My tormentors even sat me in a wooden mock up of a car with wooden doors, seats and wheels, God knows why, since it was highly unlikely that I would be driving anywhere in the foreseeable future. Fortunately, they had not yet fabricated a wooden motorcycle, since for sure, I would have fallen off and no doubt injured several members of staff in the process. Despite the humility and pain, I was determined not to stay in the hospital for one minute more than was absolutely necessary and so I persevered with the pain and accomplished their tests as best an inert lump of jelly and metal was able. For my efforts, I received a going home gift pack of goodies and an 'I've been brave' sticker, in truth it would have been more use if they had donated a similar pack from the maternity suite, the nipple lubricant and sudocreme would have been of far greater use than the articles which I received, as undoubtedly would the disposable nappies. Instead, I discovered that I was now the proud owner of a one foot high plastic toilet seat extension device. This looked like an accident waiting to happen and I guessed would result in me and the contents of my large intestine slipping off the toilet and being deposited in a heap on the bog floor, at least once there I would be able to utilize my equally incongruous freebie 'spacker stick' to clean up the resultant mess. This anomaly was a three foot long extendable grabbing device, as favoured by park keepers and litter pickers, fuck knows what the authorities deemed that I was going to accomplish with this bazaar piece of equipment. Their gift selection seemed even stranger when taking into account the fact that, at the time, my arms did not function in any way which even hinted at the notion that I was single handedly about to launch an attack on the increasingly prolific litter epidemic in the local park. Thus I used my new acquisition, as any other self respecting deviant would, and proceeded to launch an attack on Lady Langdale's rear at every opportunity, at least I didn't waste the money which the NHS had so thoughtfully expended on my behalf. The one leaving present which I did appreciate was the picnic hamper of drugs from the Pharmacy, this brightened up my days immensely. My carrier bag resembled a Columbian take away, God knows what the street value was at the time, although I would imagine that I would have been able to acquire enough money, from the local druggies, for a fortnight in Tenerife within 200 yards of leaving the main entrance of the hospital. I had Morphine in every guise possible, from the lowly tablet to patches and even phials which the patient was required to break off the tip and swallow, in short a morphine sweetie shop, the only articles which were missing were morphine lollypops and dihydrochlorine humbugs.

Since my body and brain were not on talking terms, unsurprisingly given the pain and trauma which I had subjected both of them to, and since both were in some way broken, I had to start from basics. I feel fully qualified to relate that being a middle aged baby is, in truth, no fun at all. Unlike the immature real thing, I didn't even get the benefit of being able to amuse myself with an oversized pair of baby pacifiers, not that I was mobile enough to indulge even if Melinda Messinger had offered to be my surrogate mother for the day, moreover unlike the real thing I soon discovered that at my age, soiling the bed was most definitely frowned upon. Instead, I had to amuse myself with my freebie NHS goodie bag, which those wonderful forward thinking administrators had furnished me with, and which included, I kid you not, a plastic cutlery set. Surprisingly, this was not made from the venerated Sheffield stainless steel which was invented and produced yards from the hospital, but from 'Easy grip' Chinese plastic complete with a thick handle and a bent blade and a fork, specially designed for the less able diner. Partly, because I could not control my hands and arms, but essentially because some twat had designed the utensils with a 45 degree bend, I persisted in attempting to feed myself via the wrong apertures. No matter how hard I tried I prevailed in missing my mouth and depositing my lunch in my ears, eyes or nose, as my doctor later pointed out on seeing how much weight I had lost, I obviously was not eating correctly. The fact that he came up with this revelation after removing a piece of carrot from the rear of my eye socket, I assumed would have been self explanatory. To add further insult to injury, I had to have my dinner cut up into bite size pieces, a practice which I had grown out of in my early thirties. Back then it was purely as a result of being idle, now it was a necessity. For many months, the breast feeding route seemed a whole lot simpler and more enjoyable, fortunately Lady Langdale didn't insist on me using a bib and high chair at meal times.

Since my arms were still next to useless, the daily dump became a team event, even if I had been so minded, since I had not practised the operation for several months, I most definitely could not have reached my arse, let alone wipe it. Instead each morning I would summon my ever suffering wife/personal nurse with the magic words 'I've finished dear', whereupon a pair of hands would appear and as if by magic the operation would be completed. As I became stronger and progressively regained the use of my upper body the scam became harder to pull off, until one day Lady Langdale answered my request for assistance with the words 'you can do it yourself now' to which I begrudgingly replied 'I know but I don't like'. Following a swift left hook, courtesy of Lady Langdale, from that day on I had to perform the delicate and painful operation in solitude.

Several months after leaving hospital I was laid on the settee watching TV, despite my best efforts and a whole load of physiotherapy, my left arm was still paralysed from the shoulder down to the ends of my finger tips. I became aware that I was able to move my elbow by a couple of millimetres, whilst it wasn't much it was at least a start in my rehabilitation, I called my wife to observe the spectacle, but by the time she arrived from the kitchen I was too busy crying my eyes out to explain the reason for her disturbance, this was just another small step on the road to recovery. For Neil Armstrong in 1969 it was about a step onto the surface of the moon, for me in 2007, it was about trying to wipe my own arse and hopefully, one day, be able to play a guitar again, at the time each of these goals appeared, on the balance of probability, to be unattainable dreams. Many more physiotherapy sessions, occupational health interrogations, Outpatients visits and operations followed in an attempt to rebuild me and get me back to some degree of normality, so far, most attempts at the latter have unsurprisingly failed, hardly surprising really, since I was by no means normal to start with. My frequent visits to the x-ray department have ensured that I now glow in the dark and my wife rents me out for Halloween parties as the 'dayglo spacker from hell', sometimes in the evenings she uses the glow which I emit to read a book! The excessive amounts of metal inside my body cause a host of new and interesting problems when attempting to negotiate airport security. Try explaining to an over zealous, non English speaking Thai border control officer with an ego problem and an itchy trigger finger that the bulge in your jeans is due to having a bent cock and is not in fact a 9mm pistol, after setting off the alarms on his over sensitive metal detector, especially when the officer in question later discovers enough pharmaceuticals in your luggage to restock the Bangkok branch of Boots. Believe me its odds on to initiate the rubber glove treatment and a good amount of anal rummaging.

Perhaps this scenario was the catalyst which initiated the regular nightmares to which I was becoming accustomed. Frequently I would wake up in the middle of the night sweating profusely, at least I think it was sweat, and screaming uncontrollably, whilst being convinced that I was dead or dying. Perhaps it was the effects of the Morphine or perhaps I just had a morbid fear of big handed customs officials with a latex fetish.

In truth my irrational fear of people in airport security, the little known Arsefingeraphobia, undoubtedly stemmed from my pre-accident era. In my capacity as a musician, I was en route to Tremore in South West Ireland, via Waterford airport, with the rest of the band, for a weekend music festival. If I had been sober at the time I would probably have realised that pulling the toilet door off the hinges of the small twin engined plane, in an attempt to go for a piss whilst flying at a not inconsiderable altitude, was the bad omen it eventually turned out to be. Undoubtedly the awe struck flight attendant would not have disagreed with this statement as I handed her the debris from my altercation i.e. the toilet door, neither it seemed, did the occupant of the toilet who was by now gazing out forlornly into the cabin with his trousers around his knees and a facial expression of embarrassment which bordered on shear bewilderment and mild anger. Remarkably the weekend went off without further incident until the return journey. Steve, my partner in crime, had taken the opportunity to do a spot of gift shopping for his family, I opted for the altogether more civilized option of a last Guinness in Murphy's bar before our return journey. After a brief interlude, Steve reappeared, bearing gifts.

'what you bought?' I asked, Steve proudly displayed a couple of china mugs resplendent with Labrador puppy pictures, for his parents, 'what you bought for your missus?'. After a short pause which involved Steve looking sheepishly embarrassed, he duly produced a plastic zoo set from the depths of a carrier bag, on the packaging was written, in bold type, the words 'ages three to six'. I enquired as to his twisted logic, or lack of it, which even for a brief nanosecond lead him to believe that his twenty eight year old better half would be, even in a small way, satisfied with his choice of present. His explanation for his mind numbingly stupid and naïve decision was that he didn't know what else to buy her. My assertion that a nice bottle of Chanel would undoubtedly have resulted in a higher level of bedroom action, did little to cheer him up. Not for the first time, Steve proved himself to be one of the cleverest idiots I have ever had the pleasure of knowing, a reliably stupid genius, if ever there was one. I can only assume that his mother smoked an awful lot during pregnancy, since she was only 4'6 in stilettos, this seemed to be a reasonable deduction. In an attempt too cheer up the loveable jerk, and since I have never been one to miss an opportunity for ridicule, I suggested that we should at least have a look at 'Whipsnade in a bag'. A few minutes later Murphy's bar had a small perfectly formed zoo on its surface, replete with plastic trees, plastic cages and plastic animals, with hindsight this is the point where the trouble started. It wasn't long before Steve's lack of knowledge in the ladies gift selection department was matched by his apparent zoological ineptitude and ignorance, when he duly enquired as to the identity of one of the inmates of 'Zoo Murphy'. I informed him that the small green plastic effigy in his hand was in fact an aardvark, he in turn, asserted that it was an anteater. On hearing the ensuing argument, Murphy informed the assembled throng that, in his educated opinion, the animal in question was a Tapir, this had the effect of doing sweet FA to resolve the argument but would become very relevant approximately one hour later when the question reappeared at the one and only security desk in Waterford airport. The customs official, who to this day I can only assume was a friend of Murphy's and thus was forewarned and ahead of the game, enquired of Steve, the unwilling Zookeeper, if he was taking anything out of the country which he did not have on entry. Knowing Steve, I fully expected him to reply, 'only Herpes officer' but no, in what can only be described as an outburst of complete suicidal stupidity and twatishness, Steve excelled even his own depths of total madness, as he placed his hand luggage on the x-ray belt, by replying, 'Yes officer, a plastic Zoo set'. When the officer further enquired as to what a particular item on his monitor screen was, Steve's fate was indelibly sealed. In an exhibition of pure honesty and total inanity Steve's answer was, and to this day is, quite incredible. 'I think its an anteater, Murphy reckons it's a Tapir but he says its an Aardvark'. Without waiting for further explanation the customs official promptly exited the party, Steve in one hand and a box of Latex gloves in the other, whilst uttering the unforgettable words, 'come with me sonny', Steve's feet didn't touch the floor. At this point in the proceedings, I was laid doubled up on the check in floor struggling to retain control of my bladder and giggling profusely at the spectacle which unfolded before my eyes, previously I had only witnessed scenes like this in episodes of Father Ted or Carry on films.

Eventually, after several of the longest minutes in Steve's brief time on planet Earth, he duly reappeared with a face the colour of a very embarrassed beetroot with blood pressure problems, clutching his arse in one hand and the troublesome plastic three year old's zoo kit in the other, whilst insisting that he had been violated by a middle aged customs official who had touched him in places that middle aged customs officials shouldn't. Possibly because of his newly discovered interest in anal probing or perhaps in truth because his girlfriend, like the rest of us, had no idea what the fuck to do with a small child's Irish zoo kit and did not have a clue what plastic aardvarks, anteaters and Tapirs ate, and no doubt, because she would have found a nice bottle of perfume a whole lot more acceptable, Steve was duly dumped on his return home, sad really since she had been the beneficiary of a private education and would undoubtedly have known whether the offending animal was indeed an aardvark, anteater or tapir, sadly now we will never know since she subsequently burned it along with the rest of his personal effects.

GREECE IS THE WORD

Once again I found myself sitting on an apartment balcony under an azure blue sky, on this occasion I was on the beautiful Greek island of Santorini, if, indeed, a barren dry lump of volcanic ash and donkey shit sitting in the middle of the Aegean, can be thus described. It was a hot morning in September, I welcomed the caressing cooling breeze and savoured the pipe full of 'backy' in one hand and the cool glass of local Aidani wine in the other. As I watched the condensation form on the walls of the vessel, I reflected on life and its inherent ups and downs, whilst the glass, and the table supporting it, gradually became wetter and emptier. As I observed the fleeting aerobatic display of the tiny winged African visitors, I was reminded of a learned friend's adage, which it seems is now indelibly stamped on my memory chip, as his words 'one swallow doesn't make a summer but it sure as hell makes your night', echoed between my ears. With hindsight, I should probably have filed his many such pearls of wisdom in the recycle bin, since he was also the weirdo who said 'I was having a wank the other day when the ex girlfriend came round, that's the last time I buy cheap chloroform from Lidl', not the sort of thing you want to say in front of your recently raped six year old sister over the Sunday dinner table. Apparently, the Greek equivalent of B&Q bought a job lot of typical Greek tables and paint, and the corrupt government, who probably owned B and Q, Greece, insisted that every door, window, shutter, piece of furniture, dog, cat and even the sky be painted with the ubiquitous blue colour, failing that it had to be white, probably. Peculiarly, even the cold drops of condensate which found their way down the front of my shirt and on to my hot chest, didn't piss me off, as they would have done in the UK, not that the weather was ever hot enough for the situation to present itself in darkest Rotherham. Greece has the ability to ease away the worry and stress of life and replace it with a comforting 'chill out factor', in a way that no where else on earth can emulate. The fact that the country is bankrupt and swallowing billions of Euros (and British Pounds) in the process doesn't appear to worry the Greek's in the slightest, like Oliver Twist with a bad 'coke' habit, they just keep coming back for more. The very fact that they didn't meet the entry requirements to join the Euro club, lied through their teeth and falsified every account ledger they could find, in order to be admitted, didn't seem to bother them in the least, or for that matter anybody else in Brussels. I sincerely hope that, similarly, one day, I will be able to write off my debts and never again have to bother with the time and expense of having my accounts signed off by H M Revenue and Customs, who will then hopefully insist on throwing billions of pounds in my general direction, to waste as I see fit. I expect that there is about as much likelihood of that scenario occurring as there is of Greece repaying the money which it has thus far squandered.

Whilst sitting at the bar one evening, I became involved in a less than riveting conversation with a couple from England who between them managed to tick most boxes on the list of things which I detest and avoid at all costs. It was apparent that he was an uncivil, civil servant who had a greatly exaggerated notion of his own importance and attractiveness to members of the opposite sex, seemingly, the size of his ego overshadowed the size of his manhood by some magnitude, his wife, meanwhile bordered on the arrogant teacher type and, apparently, kept a pound of plums in her mouth for emergencies, seemingly they were still in the tin. She was patently unable to straighten her little finger after years of gin and tonic abuse at the local golf club, and was the sort of stuck up bird who would undoubtedly remove the dishes from the kitchen sink before she went for a piss. They enquired as to how I intended to spend the evening. Never one to miss an opportunity to cause marital imbalance and instigate an argument, I informed them that I intended to take my wife on the quad bike, to share a bottle of wine, and watch the sunset on the rim of the caldera, at a new 'dogging site' which we had recently discovered. The blank expression on her face displayed her naivety and the fact that she was obviously not a subscriber to Dogging monthly or an adherent of the ancient Japanese dark art of deep anal penetration, she promptly

234

enquired of her husband as to the nature of the sport, whereupon, her doting pariah replied, 'it's where strangers watch each other fucking in their cars before spunking all over the windscreen, darling, you really wouldn't like it.' As I walked away from the bar she was still busy trying to scrape her bottom jaw off the patio, thus ended our brief acquaintance. Strangely, during the rest of my stay, neither one of them engaged me further in conversation, the situation was in no way eased by my habit of playing Blink 182's lilting rendition of their haunting ballad, 'I wanna fuck a dog up the arse' on the juke box, apparently they preferred to listen to the Everly brothers.

Hopefully, by the time anybody is unfortunate enough to read this drivel, Greece will be declared bankrupt and will no longer be a part of the Euro club and merkel will be fucking Sarkozy's big nose with a large 'strap on' whilst whistling Beethoven's ninth symphony in double time and spanking the cheese eating surrender monkeys arse with a large cane. Never mind the opening ceremony of the Olympic games, that would be a spectacle worthy of watching, and presumably would not cost twenty eight million pounds, either. With Greece out of the Euro and with a realistic exchange rate, middle aged curmudgeons like myself will be able to visit more cheaply and more often and support the only industry the Greeks have, apart from chain smoking and plate smashing, i.e. tourism. As I perused the landscape, spread out before me, I tried to ascertain which part of the island, I, as a British tax payer, already owned, as a result of our endless bailouts. All this despite the fact that the UK is not even in the Euro club, and is pretty much on it's own arse. In truth, the Greeks have far more pressing problems to contemplate, than the fact that they are billions of Euros overdrawn. For example,how to get young Greek children to eat olives, a feat which took myself four decades to achieve. More importantly, why in the digital age, when technological advances and nano engineering are commonplace, are the Greeks still subjected to wiping their collective arses on shiny bog roll, which is thinner than Tony Blair's sincerity, and inevitably results in the operator acquiring a shitty nail, this tends to make nose picking a whole lot less tasteful and satisfying. Unlike the rest of the known solar system, the poor sods are then obliged to deposit said remnants of paper and detritus in an unfeasibly small pedal bin which ceased to function correctly way back when Greece was still solvent and Michael Jackson was still black, and was blessed with the ability to breathe. All this inconvenience because, like the Greek government, the Greek drains are not fit for purpose. The state of the drainage system inevitably begs the question, what on earth happens in the morning, when giving a friend a dignified burial at sea, defies the laws of physics and the culprit refuses to go downhill in the time honoured manner. On the occasions when I have given birth to an oversized blind baby otter,

I don't ever recall having to kick it round the U-bend with my size nine or having to stand on the seat with a bucket of water held above my head in a vain attempt to dislodge the stubborn beast from the porcelain. Unfortunately, in Greece, this seems to be the most efficacious course of action, however it still leaves the throne bound owner contemplating how far yesterdays dinner will travel before getting stuck and bringing the entire island to a grinding halt. Perhaps this partially explains why the locals spend a large proportion of their days sitting around, smoking and drinking ouzo and coffee whilst discussing the congestion and resultant closure of various local sewers on any particular morning. I can only assume that the EU's billions have not been spent on improving the countries plumbing systems, unsurprisingly, the Santorini branch of Plumb centre went bankrupt years ago.

If after one's digital transgressions in the toilet, one feels the need to remove the debris from underneath one's finger nails, one might as well forget it. This is primarily because the local hot water producing and delivery system is about as much use as the banks and the sewerage system, in so much as it doesn't work, especially if your twattish neighbour and her entourage get to the 10ml of hot water in the heat exchanger, on the roof, before you do. This piece of apparatus is apparently even less industrious than the locals and works in a surprisingly similar way, in that, it sits in the sun all day and does 'fuck all', and inevitably results in the resident, i.e. me, having to tolerate yet another cold shower. To compound the misery, because the Greeks cannot be bothered to install shower trays or cubicles, the resultant icy fallout from the wholly inadequate shower head, which is inevitably situated so low on the wall that even a diminutive dwarf on hands and knees would struggle to get under the damned thing, then proceeds to acquaint itself with every part of the room, including walls, floors, clothes, towels, shitty pedal bins and every toilet roll within a six mile radius.

Memo to self, shitting and showering in Greece is not a pleasurable experience and is to be avoided whenever possible.

After an in-depth survey on the subject, I now feel qualified to explain why most Greek lamp posts lean at an unfeasibly dangerous angle. The Greek highway engineers use bulbs which are simply too large. This revelation I unequivocally proved whilst watching a crack team of roadside workers attempt to erect a series of new posts. They were armed with an old crow bar, a spade and the ubiquitous packet of fags, and were endeavouring to create a hole in the ground, which had been baked by the sun for decades, in which to embed the end of the lamp post. In short, they would have had more luck trying to shove a turd back up each other's arses with a spatula whilst being blindfold and having one arm tied behind their backs, i.e. none at all, undeterred, they duly persevered and eventually lowered the 30 foot pole into the inadequate 'scrape' in the earth which they had so diligently produced. Despite the shallowness of its pathetic foundations, the post was eventually erected, the fact that the only thing supporting it was a recently deposited pile of dog shit at its base did little to deter the industrious crew. Thus, my assertion that the Greek's now install unfeasibly small light fittings and bulbs in order to prevent the poles and their inadequate foundations from falling over and blocking the nations streets, anything heavier than a 9 watt eco-friendly, long life, vegetarian, tree hugging, liberal, mercury filled light bulb made from recycled lentil skins, could, and in all probability would, bring the country to its knees and spoil Stavros's and Stefano's fag and Ouzo indulgence. The ridiculous vision of a solitary half candle power light bulb attempting to illuminate the entire street appeared about as feasible as Greece not defaulting on its debt mountain again.

I did however cultivate a certain amount of sympathy for the working class Greek on my visit, after a lengthy conversation with an eloquent young student, who explained that he and his fellow country men were still expected to serve in the army for 9 months at a time, whilst earning the paltry amount of 8 Euros a day. His argument was that Greece's problems were not the fault of the ordinary working class people, rather it was the fault of the inept and corrupt politicians, civil servants and elite with open cheque books and large expense accounts, who were to blame, which caused me to reflect as to where I had witnessed a similar phenomenon before?

Whilst sitting on the terrace of an ancient winery in a quiet hillside village, miles from anywhere, I discovered, to my annoyance, that several times a week Santorini is subjected to a severe outbreak of American and Japanese tourism as the palatial cruise ships, moored in the caldera, vomit their inhabitants on to the unsuspecting isle. I still fail to understand why, when it is now possible to implant a fifty megapixel camera into a fleas right bollock, muppets still insist on travelling thousands of miles from home with a two foot long telephoto lens and a six foot long, eye gouging, fucking tripod, I can only conclude that the size of the photographic equipment is in some way exponential to the diminutive size of their brains and wedding tackle. As the tripods neared the summit of the steps to the winery, I was reminded of a scene from the film 'Zulu' as the natives attacked, or of Tommy 'going over the top' at Paschendale. The weapons neared and the droning monotones increased to fever pitch as the invasion became more imminent. Even the local cats paused from their intense genital licking session to wonder at the impromptu recreation of the assault on Iwo Jima, Greek style as the Americans ascended one side and the Japs the other, the only difference being that, on this occasion the Yanks got in first and claimed the best seats. Whilst the Jap/US invasion afforded a certain amount of entertainment, the peace and tranquillity was shattered, and my afternoons relaxation was brought to an untimely end, I returned to my apartment and the cats returned to licking their bollocks!

Perhaps like me, the local felines had long since given up on trying to comprehend the antics of our obese cousins from across the pond, a nation who after all incessantly corrupt the language which we gave them, being apparently unable to count the number of I's in aluminium, insisting on adding a Y in tomato and evidently confusing their arses and their fannies, a worrying trait especially in the bedroom department after a few large Jack Daniels. Why they insist on calling taps faucets and shamelessly steal the names of our towns and cities, frankly, shows a complete lack of imagination and downright fucking laziness of the highest order, presumably their justification for this plagiarism is that they single handedly thrashed the Germans and won the second world war on our behalf, that and the fact that they gave the world the gastronomic delights of KFC and Macdonald's, whoopee fucking doo!.

In truth, the only things on Santorini which droned louder than the Yanks were the thousands of Chinese manufactured quad bikes, which it seemed had undertaken an invasion of their own, and were quite possibly breeding somewhere on the island. These poorly engineered and even more poorly maintained, buzzing death traps were in evidence everywhere, with their droning automatic transmissions shrieking like an epileptic hooker reaching a long and tumultuous orgasm as their gearboxes struggled up and down the gear ratios in order to propel the overweight tourists and their spouses thereon, resplendent in shorts, flip flops and Ray bans.

The quieter, more sedate, traditional method of transport in Greece is the donkey, which on the whole is far more pleasing to the average ear, unless, that is, the ear in question happens to belong to the poor struggling donkey of some ten stone faced with the prospect of having to carry a sweaty obese thirty stone local with a serious body odour problem and several not inconsiderable bags of luggage up a hill in the mid day sun, for certain if the unfortunate animal had been blessed with the gift of speech he would undoubtedly have told his fat lazy owner to either loose weight, get off and walk, or buy one of those shitty Chinese quad bikes and put him in a retirement home. Just one day is all it would take to instil the finer points of animal husbandry into the fat Greek bastard's skull, simply strap the donkey and his luggage onto his more than ample torso and see how he likes it when the boot is on the other hoof, for sure in future he would treat his animals in an altogether kinder and more humane way, although I have reservations as to whether or not it would improve his personal hygiene problem. On reflection, the Greek's deserve their plumbing system, it is Gods way of rewarding lethargy and the invention of Taramasalata. As much as I enjoy Greek food, there is only so much salad, humus and feta that the human body is capable of consuming whilst maintaining the ability to produce solids.

All too soon it was time to return home to the green and pleasant land, together with 200 tattooed and sunburnt peasants and their screaming, farting and coughing offspring, for four hours of torture in cattle class at 35,000 feet. The pleasures of being cooped up in the cabin, with subhuman throwbacks, who have just spent a week drinking cheap lager, were barely ameliorated by the trend for employing ever more aged, hairy and overweight stewardesses, who appear to be getting more masculine year by year. Unfortunately the same cannot be said of their male counterparts who appear to be travelling in the opposite direction, at some point in the not too distant future, I assume that they will be able to swap clothes, names and toilets without anyone noticing. Give me back the old days when cabin crew were petite and demure and did not look like a member of the Hungarian shot-put team after an intensive course of steroids and cream doughnuts, presumably, such is the price we pay for cheap air travel.

In these days of mellow fruitlessness it is sometimes easier to reflect on life without the anger and frustrations of old and simply accept certain inevitable truths, although, you wouldn't think it after reading this shit. God hates me, local councils, MPs and HM revenue staff are a bunch of overpaid and underworked, arrogant pen pushing parasites, dentist's and doctor's receptionists think they know more than their superiors, who have the letters after their names and hold the qualifications, and inevitably they will always try to diagnose the problem themselves, rather than arrange an appointment. Strangely, they get really offended when it is explained to them in vivid expletives of less than three syllables that their job is to make the tea, clean the shithouse and answer the fucking phone to enable me to make an appointment with the real doctor, and not to enquire as to the progress of my genital warts in the waiting room, in the process. Should the patient be fortunate enough to obtain an appointment it will inevitably be for three months hence, when they have either died or the symptoms have disappeared, and will almost certainly be with a doctor whose name they cannot spell, let alone pronounce, and who speaks English so badly that the patient requires subtitles or an interpreter to comprehend the conversation.

Teachers are getting less intelligent as the education system is progressively watered down and falls apart and graduates are awarded qualifications for spelling their own names correctly. Meanwhile, judges have lost all grip of reality and have yet to learn that banning the local benefit scrounging, coke snorting, thieving alcoholic from driving for the fifteenth time that year, is not working, since he has no respect for rules and probably doesn't even own a licence or a working brain cell. The local thugs will not bother to turn up for their community based sentence because they are still pissed or stoned from the previous day's giro, and actually quite enjoy wearing an electronic tag, or simply leave it on the mantelpiece when they want to break their curfews and stick a couple of fingers up to society. The truth is that our elected representatives live in a different world from the one in which most of us are thrust and have never had a grip on reality, let alone lost it. Whilst this probably explains why they will jail the frail old pensioner for leaving her wheelie bin out on the wrong day, it in no way excuses them from giving out soft sentences to murderers and rapists or allowing illegal immigrants and foreign offenders out of custody on bail, never to be seen again.

The same inevitability tells me that, one day, world domination will be shared between the Chinese and Muslim fundamentalists, what a happy old place planet earth will be then, with their respective appreciation of an individual's rights, but at least we will not have to tolerate some unelected, overpaid Brussels' dignitary quoting the Human Rights laws every time we wish to send a murderer or rapist back to his own country, whether he owns a cat or has fortuitously impregnated his girlfriend, or both, or not. Hopefully, Belgium will be turned into a large open air penal colony for kaffirs, that is if the North Koreans haven't blown it into lower earth orbit by then, or it isn't submerged as a result of global warming and the depletion of the ice caps. For sure, England will never be any good at anything involving a ball or the Eurovision song contest, these points are unequivocal, and ones which we should have learnt by now. Simon Cowell and Chris Evans will still be talentless, filthy rich bastards who will continue to be paid disproportionately to their use to the nation.

Despite the imposition of sharia law, and a nations prayers, Sir Cliff Richard will not age and will continue to release a religious themed Christmas song for the next sixty years.

I firmly believe that Sarkozy's nose will get bigger and his height diminish with his popularity, together with Merkel's good looks, although I have no doubt that even fifty years from now the Germans will still be trying their utmost to rule the United Federal States of Europe, since they are unable to tolerate the fact that a tiny island race is still winning 2-0 on aggregate. David Cameron will still be refusing to give the electorate of broken Britain a referendum on the matter, but hopefully by then The Clegglet will have been fed to Muslim extremists in biscuit form, in a bizarre remake of the film Soylent Green, no doubt even then, he will still be hard to swallow, but perhaps then the government will actually make some decisions instead of just talking about it. The working man, few that will be left, will continue to be shafted and taxed to the hilt to pay for the ever increasing number of immigrants, wasters, criminals and scroungers, together with their welfare payments, compensation claims and cost of judicial appeals. Between them they will persist in abusing, breaking and using the law to their benefit, without a thought for anyone else, and in so doing drag the country further towards the edge of the abyss.

Probably as a result of sudden onset, post accident, nostalgia, and probably because I am ageing rapidly and long for the respectability and order of days long gone and a social structure which on the whole prevented talentless ginger radio presenters from becoming multi millionaires, I constantly find myself longing for yesterday, when I had a straight cock and a mind and body which functioned as per the user manual. When it was not imperative for a three year old child to possess a three hundred pound state of the art mobile telecommunication device in order that they could watch porn and send pictures of their developing genitalia to Uncle Frank in Hamburg. A time when the only telephones that we had had numbers that we could remember and were located on a street corner or on a shelf at the bottom of the stairs and for which the prospective user was required to put ten pence in the piggy bank for the pleasure of its use, especially if one's parents were standing by eavesdropping and checking for payment, a time when cameras contained films and instant Polaroid pictures only cost twenty quid a shot, which, no doubt, cost Uncle Frank a small fortune. Sometimes it is good to reminisce to a time when the Grand Prix was interesting and not merely a procession of spoilt rich kids, when motor racing was dangerous and, more importantly, when sex was safe, instead of vice versa. When the licence holder had to decide which one of the three channels to watch on TV, in glorious black and white, on a low definition, twelve inch screen, although in truth there was still more watchable viewing material broadcast than on the hundreds of channels available today. In those days the gas board, GPO, and the electric board did what it said on the tin, if there was a problem you knew exactly who to call and every couple of months the board would send a nice man wearing a suit and tie round to read the meter, invariably, he was who he said he was and did not need to carry photo ID, more importantly, he would not enter your house and proceed to rob you of anything worth nicking or physically violate your youngest daughter on a random orifice basis, nor did he reside in the Indian sub continent and telephone you at 7.30 on a Sunday morning if you happened to be a nanosecond late with a payment. Back then the arrogant money grabbing bastards did not expect the consumer to do the job themselves, nor did they furnish the customer with an estimated bill when they couldn't be bothered to read the meter and then threaten to kill his kids and burn down his house when he refused to pay a vastly inflated, fictitious ransom for the privilege of having lighting and heating, although, if my memory serves me correctly sometimes these luxuries were only available for limited hours for three days per week. Moreover the companies were British and owned by the people, back then they were not responsible for sending billions of pounds out of the country to parent companies and shareholders in France, Germany and Russia, mainly because we were still bombing them and kicking their arses, or at any rate preparing to do so. In those halcyon days Great Britain rightly had a proud industrial heritage, it's population considered it normal to work for a living and did not expect to sit on their fat arses watching daytime TV and being paid by the state for the privilege, in those days we produced more than lying politicians and bent greedy bankers, and our steel, ships, bikes and cars, not to mention textiles, chemicals and an aero industry which was the envy of the world, were exported to each of its corners, which incidentally, we also owned. Back then, the only thing that the Chinese built were useless armies of clay soldiers and ridiculously long walls, whilst living on a diet of rice and fatty meat with jam on! Similarly, the cars we drove, were invariably made in Britain, when the factories were not on strike, and, although they would invariably decompose the first time that it rained, leaving a pile of red oxide and oil, were about as streamlined as Hattie Jacques after an 'eat all you can' buffet, and would constantly break down at the most inopportune times, at least the owner could service them and work on them himself without a degree in advanced computing and astrophysics, furthermore it did not cost the equivalent of a week's wages in fuel to pop down to Tesco for the weekly shop, principally because hardly anybody north of Watford had heard of the monopolistic, retailing bastards and we still had a multitude of friendly corner shops at our disposal who exuded what used to be known as 'customer service'.

In those days, everyone knew their neighbours along the whole street, they didn't bother to lock their doors when they went next door to borrow a cup of sugar, they didn't need to since, back then, the local gippos sold heather, sharpened knives or collected scrap. Today a trip next door is most likely to result in a knife in the neck from a failed asylum seeker on Methadone, and the pikeys simply help themselves to the lead and copper, whether it is been used or not, then spend the proceeds on mansions and massive 4 x 4's and have the audacity to cite the laws of the land, which ordinarily they break on a daily basis, to prevent their eviction from Dale Farm and other such illegal camps, whilst squandering millions of pounds of tax payers money, to which they undoubtedly will not have contributed, on legal aid and appeals, in the process.

When Britain was great, and hospitals smelt of hospitals and were clean, when everybody knew that choir boys and children in care were getting bummed ,but kept the fact quiet, whilst the

Catholic church pretended that abortions only occurred in darkest Africa, where the blacks used to live, and the more backward corners of Walsall, where they now do. Where Sir Jimmy Savile was still considered to be a saint and the sort of man you would like to call 'uncle', especially since he answered your letter and fixed it for you to be blindfolded and milk a cow.

Britain's armed forces were respected and their numbers easily outnumbered the membership of the WI, we considered that we were posh and living the high life if we could afford a Vesta packet meal, bottle of brown ale and a bar of chocolate, on a Saturday night, and we were content to watch inane crap such as 'The Black and White minstrel show' or 'It's a Knockout'. Long before my hair turned grey, play stations were not bought on line from Amazon but had two legs and breasts and were played with behind the bike sheds, during fag breaks. Mothers knitted and sewed clothes, since they could not afford designer labels, these same garments were then invariably handed down to the next generation, unfortunately, in my case, this meant that I ended up wearing my sister's skirts and dresses, which caused serious issues in later life, but which, fortunately, I have now outgrown, except on alternate Tuesdays. Still, I maintain that what a man does in the comfort of his own attic is his business.

Obviously, there is a limit as to how far back in our social history, it would be prudent to regress. I would not for example expect the poor to live in a cold, stark workhouse, whilst dining on gruel and passing the hours picking bubonic plague scabs from off of their faces, unless that is, they happened to be disgraced members of parliament or council pen pushers. On reflection, it is possibly no longer socially acceptable to force small children up chimneys, even if they were caught trying to sell MDMA to their baby sister. Back when times were good it didn't matter, since invariably they had another dozen siblings to replace them, twenty if they were Catholic, when they died from some pernicious form of lung disease. Similarly, back then it was acceptable to play conkers with rats and 'poo sticks' with real shit in open sewers, similarly, it was not taboo to use children with Rickets as croquet hoops.

Fortunately, as is patently obvious, I no longer concern myself with such trivial matters, preferring as I do, to concentrate on keeping control of my bodily functions and practising my anal hygiene. Every day is a struggle to survive, recover to something like my former self, and defeat the constant physical and mental pain, but hey! I'm still breathing, still pissing off the local traffic warden every time I use my blue badge, and still thanking any god anywhere that my wonderful wife was there to get me through.

The way I see it, I've had five years more than I deserved, and whilst sometimes it doesn't feel that way, I consider myself pretty lucky to be able to watch the sun rise one more time on our wonderful, if fucked, planet. At least, I still get to enjoy the good things in life like analgesia, toothache and prostate inspections, whilst it is not always easy, if I didn't try then I would go mad, I'd really hate that!

Thanks for the rant,

Regards Martyn.

AND ANOTHER THING!

Day three of my, self inflicted, internment in Stalag 41 in the demilitarised zone of Gran Canaria , or as Mr Tompson, as ever frugal with the details of his synopsis, euphemistically describes his run down hotel in his eminent work of fiction and bullshit that is his brochure, the upmarket resort of Tourito in the south of the island, i.e. the arse end, for sure he would have made a better estate agent than package holiday magnate, one can only presume that he missed his calling as an eminent politician of our generation, such are his abilities at lying out of his arse vent. Disregarding the weekly prison bus service to the airport, the only way into this sun kissed shrine to obesity and aged mediocrity, was apparently by abseiling or base jumping from the all encompassing cliff faces which formed the outermost extremities of the penitentiary, similarly   ,the only way out appeared to be via recourse to a body bag and a death certificate, just how easy these criteria were to obtain I would only discover after sampling the woeful levels of neglect and hygiene standards of Manuel Del Bastardo and his fellow guards. Since I had neglected to pack my pitons, ropes, karabiners and designer body bag, escape seemed to be strictly limited to the prison courier bus, some seven days hence, it seemed obvious to my cynical mind that the term 'all inclusive' referred to the internees and not the level of service on offer, the large dayglo flag on the beach in front of the hotel, which advertised the local water sports emporia, pretty much hit the nail on the head in four letters, it simply said DIVE.

With the benefit of hindsight, I should have recognised the signs of forthcoming trouble, the moment that I set foot in the hotel's reception. Experience has taught me that any establishment that offers Sanatogen on draught and has Steradent and denture fixative paste dispensers in place of condom machines and vibrating knob accessories in the gents, tends to cater for the older members of society whose next holiday abroad is more likely to be a one way trip to a Dignitas suite in Zurich than an 18-30's rave/drug orientated holiday to Ibiza. It is usually a foregone certainty that the evenings dancing and revelry will more closely resemble an out take of Zombie Flesh Eaters Two than a rehearsal for Hot Gossip's mid seventies routines. This fact was more than evident when I became engrossed by the 'fuller figured', German sausage devouring champion, circa 1936, who was firmly ensconced, together with her towels and sun bed, by the pool. I realised, somewhat belatedly and embarrassingly that I had been gazing, a little too obviously it seemed, at her enormous belly button hernia for an inordinate amount of time. To say that it was large enough to feed a large and very hungry family on a Sunday lunch time, would not have been stretching the truth to any degree. It sat, like a giant volume control in the middle of her stomach as if waiting for its owner to feed it a bag of crisps. For years I have been secretly proud of the fact that I could spot a naked pair of breasts or an errant nipple at a distance of two hundred metres or more, but here is the point, I was so enrapt with the wayward bulge, that I did not even notice that it's owner was wearing nothing apart from a bootlace up her, not insignificant, arse crack, in truth this was partially because her equally large nipples and base plates were laying on the patio on either side of the sun lounger, but even so the experience serves to highlight the dangers, to serious admirers of the female form, of hanging around for any length of time in God's waiting room.

Fortunately, as the old adage goes, every cloud had a silver lining this particular nebular respite involved the presentation of the daily awards for the 'in house' sporting activities. Since there did not appear to be any honours on offer for imbibing the highest intake of undrinkable witch piss wine or tasteless flat lager, I was sadly exempt from the celebrations. Instead I had to console myself with the riveting entertainment of the proceedings. In what I can only conclude was an ill conceived plan to avoid paying for carers or child minding facilities on behalf of the parents, most of the awards seemed to go to the hotel's pet mong. Somewhat bizarrely the guardians of this inept window licker had entered the poor incumbent into every conceivable discipline, I sat and wondered, with not a small amount of bemusement, at the prudence of arming the poor retard with a bow and arrow and even more astonishingly, a rifle. Somehow, my brain was telling me that wax crayons or a sand pit would have been more appropriate. Amazingly, in a graphic display of incompetence, obesity and senility on the part of the rest of the myopic contestants, the mong promptly won both events, without it seemed killing or maiming anybody in the process, although with the benefit of hindsight, the untimely demise of the pair of six month old twins who insisted on imitating the mating calls of an irate African Grey parrot at meal times, would not have been an inconsolable loss, I concluded that it was a pity, to anyone with a passing interest in peace and tranquillity, that the screaming pair of nauseating, nappy filling bastards were not conjoined at the mouth, not only would this have kept them quiet but it would also have made them a larger target for the sharp shooting mong to be able to inflict life threatening injuries. Frankly, I was glad that I was not within range of her extensive arsenal at the time, furthermore, in what can only be regarded as gross negligence on behalf of the organizers, it transpired that the potential bloodbath was enacted adjacent to the children's playground, on reflection the rep in charge did bear more than a passing resemblance to Ian Brady, poor girl. Just when I determined that the inane act of providing lethal weapons to the poor unfortunate could not escalate in the comedy war game stakes, the following day's events saw the champion 'marks mong' being given free range of a set of darts, it appeared that if it was sharp or in any way inherently dangerous, some devious degenerate with a sick sense of the macabre in Mr T's head office, thought that it would occupy the bipedal vegetable and prevent her from harassing the other guests, whilst in the process provide hours of fun for all concerned. Surely it would have been easier, and a whole lot safer, to lick her lips and affix her to the plate glass windows which adorned the front of the hotel for the duration of the proceedings, in truth, I half expected to see her at the airport on the return leg of the journey wing walking naked on a 737 whilst juggling scimitars blindfolded and pouring neat vodka shots into her eye sockets, for sure if there was an award for the largest collection of chromosomes our reluctant heroine would most definitely have been taking home another certificate to hang on her cage wall. Later, I observed that the following day's activities included ping pong, however, in the interests of retaining what little remained of my sanity and in a vain attempt to preserve a certain amount of decorum, I decided to omit this spectacle from my day's schedule, the thought of a semi prone mong honing her ballistics prowess by recourse to her front bottom and various other assorted orifices in the direction of a target half way up the wall of the children's playground, I deemed to be a step too far and probably better left to the imagination, although it would undoubtedly have made for better entertainment than the resident

Spanish tribute to the Beatles who insisted on trying to emulate their heroes with a most unconvincing attempt at what must surely be the world's worst sounding accent. Manuel Macca sounded more akin to an asthmatic Pakistani with nasal polyps and a sore throat following a badly botched tracheotomy operation, than anybody from the hub cap nicking capital of the UK, and merely served to convince me that, like the residents of Liverpool, the band's time would have been better spent learning to speak English.

'Don't flush the shithouse' I shouted to Lady Langdale, her bemused scowl apparently required an explanation, 'I've disconnected it, it's where I am going to start the tunnel to get us out of this dump', I replied. The thought of spending a week without parole confined in a concrete cell was not one which I relished with any amount of enthusiasm, unfortunately, my plan was doomed from its inception since we were located some six stories up in the concrete monstrosity, or as it was described by Mr T, 'home from home', I can only conclude that his home is a badly built, characterless shithole at the arse end of the back of beyond which smells of blocked drains and human excrement. To make matters worse, the only utensils to hand were a bottle opener, tea spoon and a ballpoint pen which I reasoned would be pretty ineffectual at dealing with reinforced concrete floors, even if it was cast by inept, lazy Spanish builders.

The hotel resembled a downmarket Billy Butlin's establishment with sunshine, it was thirteen unlucky stories high and was skilfully crafted into the imposing sheer rock face, in truth the monstrosity made Sheffield's Hyde Park flats, a place not exactly renowned for its inherent aesthetic prowess, where throwing TV sets off balconies at babies in pushchairs is the local past time and unemployment is compulsory, look appealing, this fact only serves to illustrate the deficiencies in the hotel's architects vision and design abilities. Unfortunately the builders skill did not, as far as I could see, extend to any form of damp proofing qualifications, which went some way towards explaining the peeling paint on the walls and ceilings and the pervading odour of shit, alas it was not possible to go outside in order to partake of some fresh air since this was likewise similarly affected and the air was not of the sweetest quality, a walk along the artificial beach, all two hundred yards of it, was sadly, unlikely to bring relief to one's sinuses, seemingly, there was nothing artificial about the smell despite it no doubt being man made. The beach, unlike the hotel, was at least swept regularly.

Initially, I insisted that Lady Langdale deposit the spoil from my tunnel digging exploits in the hotel grounds, this she accomplished by fashioning a pair of leg bags from the curtains in the room which she emptied via a drawstring and deftly spread their contents around the borders, however closer examination of the dirt already strewn about the floors inside showed this to be a waste of time and henceforth she dumped the fruits of my labours with the rest of the amassed detritus, nobody seemed to notice and I don't recall the cockroaches complaining, unless they did so in Spanish. Since our room was located half way up the building and thus had a readymade launch site, it would, on reflection, have been easier to fashion an escape glider from a couple of sun loungers and bed sheets doped with the abundant supply of undercooked eggs on offer each breakfast. If I had, I have no doubt that the in flight service would also have been a great improvement on Mr T's half hearted attempt of micro waved chav food, and for sure there would have been no screaming uncontrollable brats sat behind me during my descent to freedom. Neither, I reasoned, would I have to endure the insipid, arrogant, wob eyed little shit of a five year old girl with a speech impediment enlightening me, via the in house video screens, as to the finer points of the safety routine and escape routes on Mr T's Boeing sourced taxi. It is a sad and parlous fact that there is never a deviant Radio One DJ around when they could serve some useful purpose, for sure, I for one, would be far more interested in watching her patronising performance in HD format whilst attempting to gargle with big Jim's member stuck half way down her arrogant little throat, I venture to suggest that she would not be so bloody smug then, nor would she be clamouring to film Safety Routine Two, the sequel in a hurry.

Whilst admiring Manuel's building techniques and prowess, I was struck by the fact that he was obviously oblivious to the phenomena that is the right angle. The hotel was apparently constructed without recourse to a single one, although, on occasions he and his crew came close, the elusive right angle was conspicuous by its absence. It appeared that Manuel had used something more akin to my own exceedingly bent member than anything resembling a set square. For sure the square on Manuel's hypotenuse did not equal the sum of the squares on the two opposite sides any more than Frau Hernia resembled a young Kate Moss, personally I just hoped that his creation remained standing long enough for me to vacate its confines.

For sure, my next foray to warmer climes will be to somewhere more welcoming such as a Syrian city break or a pirate based sabbatical cruise around the Somalian coastline.

Reviews

Having read this pile of shit, it is obvious that this man is exaggerating the extent of Gainsborough's problems. The four staff in our office had a count and, between us, we only have 47 fingers and 49 toes. Moreover, a recent poll of local school leavers showed that the number of pupils leaving full time education who 'were thick as fuck', was far nearer 97% than the 98% claimed. (Gainsborough town press secretary, extract from his article, 'This cunts talking bollocks out of his arse'.)

He made me touch him and he fucking enjoyed it no matter what the liar says, he was gagging for it. (Customs official (ret'd)Waterford airport 2006, ps it was an aardvark.)

This work is clearly a thinly veiled attack on the vulnerable law abiding minority of the population who make their living in the peg dealing, tarmacing, thieving, scrap nicking, above the law, ignorant, illiterate, heather picking, travelling sector of society. I was only on the dole for eleven months last year, although to be fair I was 'on holiday' in a Wakefield top security all inclusive hotel for the remainder. (Mr A. Smith, caravan 2, Dale Farm, Cambridge, Editor Practical Caravanning and thieving, 2008).

I laughed so much that I pissed myself! It's not that funny but I really enjoyed his tales of misery, suffering, pain and bad luck. Pete said he hasn't laughed so much since the Japanese tsunami, and his mum trapped her tit in the mangle. (God, supreme editor in chief, War cry.)

Such a bag of wank, I have never had the misfortune to read before. He is clearly lying out of his arse, my wife is 5' 10" high and only 5' 8" wide, and she doesn't even like after eight mints. (National Westminster Bank manager. (Ret'd).

Do not believe a fucking word this man says, he is a fucking liar and so is his dog (A local grey haired pensioner and regular Tesco shopper).

This is the funniest thing wot I have ever read, it's even better than Woman's Weekly, if only he had included a couple of knitting patterns and a crossword. (Mrs Langdale, mother.)

What a total wanker, I always knew that he was responsible for the sticky pages in my newspapers, which is why I installed the camera in his bedpost. (Mr Langdale senior, father).

We would like to emphasise that we do not recommend Swarfega as a sexual lubricant as it is highly corrosive and may contain nuts. (MD Swarfega Detergent monthly 2008) PS I suggest using Utterly Butterly, it slides better and has lower cholesterol.

Under no circumstances should our condoms be used as liquid filled projectiles, especially the chocolate flavoured ones, without the relevant risk assessment, insurance and ballistics licence. Following your information, we have forwarded the repair bill for the vending machine to South Yorkshire Police. (Mr Onyer-Toole MD. LRC.)

I object most strongly to the foul and offensive language used in this piece of shit literature. The twatting bastard responsible should learn how to use the Queens English fucking proper. (name and address supplied).

This book is deeply offensive to the Catholic church, not all bishops are gay arse bandits, I know of at least two who are not. Furthermore they assure me that they have never stuck their cocks up a choirboy's bum hole. I fully endorse the ordaining of female bishops, it opens up a whole new field of depravity for the more liberal minded clergyman.

Our lager is not as shit as this lying bastard makes out, I have got pissed on it on several occasions.(Mr Maidenswee CEO Carling).

Where's my fucking dinner! (Wilf).

Printed in Great Britain
by Amazon